MW01484245

'In an era where digital transformation often feels like a race to outpace disruption, *Resurgent* reminds us that true resilience comes from aligning technological progress with purpose. Birkinshaw and Fallon show that established companies can thrive not by clinging to the past, but by embracing change as a force for good – creating value not just for shareholders, but for society and the planet. A must-read for leaders determined to be net positive in the digital age.'

Paul Polman, business leader, investor, philanthropist

'*Resurgent* offers a masterful analysis of the challenges and opportunities presented by digital transformation, and a comprehensive guide on how established organizations can harness the power of digital disruption to emerge stronger and more competitive. For organizations facing the relentless pace of technological change, *Resurgent* is an invaluable resource and a roadmap to navigating its complexities with confidence and agility.'

Pascal Finette, founder and CEO, be radical

'In these tumultuous times, Birkinshaw and Fallon give us a roadmap for understanding how to harness the opportunities created by digital transformation. In it, they have a particular message for incumbent firms: AI doesn't have to be a death sentence, but it will require business model innovation and not just technological adaptation.'

Sarah Kaplan, Professor of Strategic Management at the University of Toronto's Rotman School of Management

'Amidst all the change and disruption, *Resurgent* tells a story of optimism and resilience. It is possible for incumbents to respond successfully to disruption and the book provides a clear roadmap on how to do it with real examples to back up its ideas and recommendations. This wonderful book should be required reading for any senior executive whose industry or company is facing disruptive change.'

Costas Markides, Professor of Strategy and Entrepreneurship and holder of the Robert Bauman Chair in Strategic Leadership, London Business School

'*Resurgent* is not only a cracking read but a valuable leadership guide on how to embrace change and transform even the most traditional of businesses. Building on years of practical experience, it provides pragmatic advice that will resonate with anyone who has been at the helm of an organization in a constantly changing environment.'

Christine Hodgson, Chair, Severn Trent Plc

'In today's turbulent times, this book offers welcome advice for senior leaders everywhere. It is an important reminder that all companies, including industry leaders like Royal Bank of Canada, despite huge benefits of scale and incumbency, cannot take our success for granted. We need to have the humility to ask, what are we missing? And we need to have the courage to respond in a bold and agile way.'

Doug Guzman, Deputy Chairman, Royal Bank of Canada

'How do industry incumbents embrace digital transformation? How do you simplify your business and serve your customers better? Where do you place your big bets and embrace new business models? How do you tell a compelling story through often challenging times? And how do you lead when there is so much internal resistance to change? With compelling data, case studies and personal stories, Birkinshaw and Fallon show how established companies can fight back and win through an age of digital disruption. As we all embrace the new age of AI, this essential road map to survival could not be more timely.'

Gavin Patterson, former CEO, BT Group plc and former
Chief Revenue Officer, Salesforce.

'*Resurgent* dispels the myth that disruption inevitably dooms established firms, revealing how incumbents can leverage their strengths and adaptability to succeed. With candid stories and a roadmap for confident digital transformation, this book is a must-have for business leaders, consultants, and students.'

Doug Murphy, former President and CEO, Corus Entertainment

Resurgent

How established organizations can
fight back and thrive in an age
of digital transformation

Julian Birkinshaw
and John Fallon

with Adam Bouzelmate

BLOOMSBURY BUSINESS
LONDON · OXFORD · NEW YORK · NEW DELHI · SYDNEY

BLOOMSBURY BUSINESS
Bloomsbury Publishing Plc
50 Bedford Square, London, WC1B 3DP, UK
Bloomsbury Publishing Ireland Limited,
29 Earlsfort Terrace, Dublin 2, D02 AY28, Ireland

A catalogue record for this book is available from the British Library

Library of Congress Cataloguing-in-Publication data has been applied for

ISBN: HB: 978-1-3994-2201-7; eBook: 978-1-3994-2200-0

2 4 6 8 10 9 7 5 3 1

Typeset by Deanta Global Publishing Services, Chennai, India
Printed and bound in Great Britain by CPI Group (UK) Ltd, Croydon CR0 4YY

MIX
Paper | Supporting
responsible forestry
FSC
www.fsc.org   FSC® C013604

To find out more about our authors and books visit www.bloomsbury.com
and sign up for our newsletters

For product safety related questions contact productsafety@bloomsbury.com

To Della, Lorna and Ellie. And to all my colleagues over the years at Pearson and in the wider world of education. Always learning…

John Fallon

To Laura, Ross, Duncan and Lisa – thanks for embracing our transatlantic lifestyle!

Julian Birkinshaw

To Mum, Dad, Anis and Yasmin – thank you for all that you have done and for all your support.

Adam B. Bouzelmate

CONTENTS

ACKNOWLEDGEMENTS

This book follows an online course we created called Leading Digital Transformation. This is offered through London Business School (LBS) directly and a version of it can also be found on the Coursera platform (www.coursera.org). We first started teaching the LBS course in early 2023. We then rewrote and augmented the content of the course to create this book, published in July 2025.

In developing the course and the book, we interviewed a range of senior executives and related figures who have led digital transformation across a range of large companies, mainly drawn from the media sector. They are Jeremy Darroch, Catherine Faiers, Albert Hitchcock, Madeline McIntosh, Gavin Patterson, Annette Thomas, Patrick Wellington, Coram Williams, John Behrens, Tim Bozik and Danny Attias. The quotes attributed to them that are included throughout this book are taken from those interviews. We thank them for giving so generously of their time and for sharing their experiences and insights. Other than the words we attribute directly to them, all the views and opinions expressed in the book are, of course, ours alone.

We would also like to thank our colleagues at the London Business School – and the students in our classes – with whom we have debated and tested these ideas over the last four years. Our special thanks to Oded Koenigsberg – who first introduced us to each other – and Costas Markides. John would also like to thank colleagues at Northeastern University and the D'Amore-McKim School of Business at Northeastern University, who have also helped to hone and shape his thinking.

Finally, Adam Bouzelmate played a vital role in getting this book in shape. Adam was in one of Julian's MBA classes at London Business School and he stood out as one of the most insightful and well-read students in the class. He put in countless days of effort on the book, first turning our video transcripts into readable text and then working with us to sharpen up our arguments. Given all the other calls on our time, we simply wouldn't have found the time to pull this book together without Adam's help, so we are happy to give him due credit on the cover of this book.

Julian Birkinshaw and John Fallon

INTRODUCTION

Digital transformation (DT) is a never-ending process. Over the last 50 years we lived through the first wave of computerization in the 1970s and 1980s and then the internet era of the 1990s and 2000s. These were followed by mobile revolution of the 2010s, inspired by the invention of the iPhone, and the virtual revolution of 2020, triggered by a global pandemic. Then in November 2022, ChatGPT was launched and the next round of change – the Generative AI revolution – was underway.

Writing this book at the end of 2024 means there is still a lot of uncertainty about how Generative AI will play out. In terms of speed of consumer adoption, level of corporate investment and overall media attention it is already huge – at least on a par with the internet and smartphone revolutions. Some observers have gone even bigger. According to former Microsoft CEO Bill Gates, it has 'the potential to change the world in ways that we can't even imagine'. Computer scientist Ray Kurzweil predicts that 'by the time children born today are in kindergarten, AI will probably have surpassed humans at all cognitive tasks from science to creativity'. Others are more cautious, noting the limitations and risks of this new technology, and recognizing the enduring truth of Amara's Law: we tend to overestimate the effect of technology in the short run and underestimate the effect in the long run (we discuss this further in Chapter 2).

The best way to make sense of Generative AI's potential is to provide some perspective. The technology itself is completely new, but the way consumers respond to it and the market dynamics between startups and incumbents are likely to echo what has gone before: the more things change, the more they stay the same. That is what this book is all about.

More specifically, the book focuses on how established firms have already adapted to earlier waves of digital change and how they are positioning themselves to change again as the Generative AI revolution unfolds. And it's a tale of optimism and resilience. Unlike many observers who see established firms being driven out by technological change, we see them as resurgent – proactive and capable of reviving themselves in the face of new competitive forces.

John has spent his entire business career grappling with digital technology. He was CEO of Pearson Corporation between 2012 and 2020, a period of huge upheaval in the education and media industry, and he oversaw – among many other things – the shift in the college textbook industry to a digital-first model.

Julian worked at London Business School for more than 25 years, researching, teaching and consulting on digital technology for businesses around the world. He led major change initiatives to create online and blended learning activities there. Now, he is embracing similar challenges as the Dean of Ivey, Canada's leading business school.

We began working together in late 2021 as the world began to recover from the Covid pandemic and we found common ground in our somewhat cautious perspective on the technology hype that was going on around us. This was the year that Apple, Google, Amazon and Microsoft first reached trillion-dollar valuations and when every tech stock or tech-enabled company was getting record valuations. Companies as varied as Zoom, Stripe, Klarna, 2U, Chegg, Coinbase and Peleton were trading at vast multiples of sales revenues.

To be sure, we weren't disputing the growing importance of digital technology to the global economy, nor were we doubting the stranglehold the big-tech companies (Microsoft, Amazon, Apple, Google) had gained on our everyday lives. What was missing was a sense of proportionality; the narrative in the business press was *all* about tech. Companies in the traditional parts of the economy, from energy to industrial to consumer goods to travel to health, rarely got a mention. Everyone was talking about the disrupters – the startups and the entrepreneurs – and not about the incumbents. We thought it was time for a reality check. Here is John's story first…

THE BIG BETS CONFERENCE

In October 2017, I was one of 100 global company CEOs gathered in Brooklyn, New York. We were drawn from 17 different industries. Together, our companies made $2 trillion in annual revenues. We were meeting to share the 'big bets' we were making on our digital future. We were very focused on how we were going to survive and prosper in the so-called second machine age, a new industrial revolution brought about by a fusion of technologies blurring the lines between the physical and digital spheres.

We were all big, mature, profitable cash-generative businesses and the market leaders in our fields, with brands and products admired around the world. We weren't averse to change – most of our companies had been in existence for 50 years or more, constantly adopting new technologies and new ways of working. Already we used technology at scale to automate our production and run our enterprises. Most of us also had a well-established online presence and some success in launching new digital products and services. But, almost without exception, talk of the second machine age was making us feel anxious and vulnerable. My company, Pearson, was in the middle of a particularly challenging digital transformation, but I sensed I wasn't the only CEO in the room feeling that their business was unloved, undervalued and under pressure.

For Phase 1 of this new digital revolution had been all about the platform effect. It had been won decisively by a new generation of companies – at the time known as the FAANGS (Facebook, Amazon, Apple, Netflix, Google, Salesforce). These relatively young companies had built out the new global platforms, growing very quickly, generating huge profits and mountains of cash. They also commanded huge market valuations in the expectation they had the platform, the ambition and the firepower to go on and seriously disrupt our own industries.

These platform companies had, in turn, spawned ecosystems of well-funded, highly valued and super-hyped new entrants. The new entrants didn't have to worry about many of the things that we did – a large customer base still dependent on our analogue products, legacy infrastructure, making a profit, meeting short-term earnings expectations. These new entrants were burning through lots of cash, focusing obsessively on innovation and growth as they set about disrupting our industries, destroying our business models, luring away our talent and our customers and wrenching away our often long-standing and hard-won incumbencies. And yet as we discerned some common themes in the 'Big Bets' we were each making in our own digital transformations, the mood in the meeting changed from suppressed anxiety to first defiance and then growing confidence for at the core of our companies are capabilities and qualities that remain highly relevant to the digital age. We are market leaders for a reason – we know our customers and our markets well, and we have great product, sales and marketing expertise. Operationally savvy and financially strong, we have deep insights into our areas of expertise that no one else has, giving us some big competitive advantages.

For example, if Phase 1 of the digital revolution was about the platform effect, Phase 2 is all about harnessing the power of all the knowledge – the data – unleashed by those platforms and the emerging technologies of artificial intelligence (AI) and machine learning. By far the most valuable data is the 80 per cent of proprietary information that sits within the world's leading companies and emerges from our daily interactions with many millions of customers around the world, who choose our products and services for most aspects of daily life. Our job is to use that data in innovative ways to the benefit of our customers.

We came to a clear conclusion: we incumbents are not going quietly into that dark night. This will not prove to be our Kodak moment. We're not going the way of Nokia or BlackBerry, of Blockbuster or Borders: we know that success is precarious, that we have no natural birth right to lifelong profitability. We will need to jettison our analogue baggage and infrastructure and embrace digital transformation. It will be disruptive and difficult because growth, like history, doesn't run in a straight line. But we are going to meet the needs of our customers today and disrupt and innovate our way to a better light. We are going to survive; and we are going to prosper. We gave our meeting a new name: Big Bets became Incumbents Strike Back.

This was John's experience back in 2017 and events over the subsequent seven years showed that the CEOs he rubbed shoulders with at the Big Bets conference were mostly right to be optimistic. As we will discuss over the course of this book, many incumbents have caught up with technology innovators, they have capitalized on their existing strengths and they have become smarter and more agile in how they cope with digital change.

Of course, none of this is to deny the spectacular growth of the big technology companies. At the time of writing, the top tech companies often referred to as the magnificent seven (Alphabet, Amazon, Apple, Meta, Microsoft, Nvidia, Tesla) had a combined market capitalization of around $11 trillion, greater than the gross domestic product (GDP) of every country in the world except the US and China, and bigger than the combined market capitalizations of all the stock markets in Japan, Canada and the UK. None of the traditional incumbents has broken out in the way the magnificent seven have, but they have overwhelmingly found a way through, surviving and increasingly prospering through a time of exponential change, while many of the venture capital-backed disruptors of the last decade have collapsed in value.

UNICORNS AND DINOSAURS

Julian, from his own vantage point as an academic, saw the same issues but at a higher level of abstraction. His research on this topic was published in *Harvard Business Review* in 2022 and was voted the best article in that year.[1] It started as follows:

> *The prevailing narrative in business today is one of ever-faster change and creative destruction. Big Tech companies are taking over, the number of unicorns keeps growing, the average tenure of old-economy companies on the S&P 500 is plummeting, and incumbency has never been worth less.*

The article argued that from a big-picture perspective, the reality was more nuanced, with many sectors of the economy experiencing remarkably *low* levels of disruption.

Consider the following data point. The internet revolution started in the mid-1990s, over a quarter century ago, long enough for the winds of change to work their way through the whole economy. So how many of the Fortune 500 in 2024 didn't exist back in 1995?

This is not a rhetorical question! Stop reading, get a pen and paper out and write down a number. We have done this exercise with countless groups of executives and students. Most people of course have no idea, but it's fascinating to see how huge the range of answers is. We reckon the median answer, from people we have asked, is around 200 (with a big variance). In other words, people imagine that about two-fifths of the Fortune 500 consists of relatively young companies that were created during or after the internet revolution.

It turns out the true answer is 24. The other 476 have all been around, in some shape or form, since before 1995. There is often an audible gasp from the room when we present this fact.

It's useful to unpack this data, to show what is actually happening to the Fortune 500 and to explain why most people's expectations are so out of line with reality. The boxed text provides the details of this analysis but the key point is that we have some myths to dispel. Three, in particular.

Myth: Every sector is under threat.
Reality: Some industries have been affected very significantly by the digital revolution. TMT (telecom, media, technology) is of course the most affected, but retailing has also seen major disruption, largely because Amazon has been so successful. Some industries have seen pockets of disruption (for example, payments in banking), but many industries have been hardly affected at all. Industrial companies, energy, consumer goods and even health and banking have seen enormous amounts of stability in terms of the Fortune 500 make-up. For example, there were 57 industrial companies (including autos and aerospace) in the Fortune 500 in 1995 and there are 57 today, at the time of writing. Only one – Tesla – is less than 30 years old.
Myth: Disruption happens quickly and is accelerating.

Reality: Disruption usually takes a long time to play out. There are a couple of exceptions to this rule – for example, Blockbuster Video went from market leader to bankruptcy in about four years, and Nokia and BlackBerry were killed off by the iPhone in less than three years. But most industries evolve at a much slower pace. The transition to digital imaging in photography took about 20 years to play out. The shift in the music industry, from album-buying to streaming, took 15 years. Retail banking started to change in the mid-1990s with internet banking, but 30 years on, it is still in the throes of change and the big players are still the same as ever. Insurance, auditing, law and healthcare have arguably taken even longer to feel the effects of the digital revolution. And it is not just digital technology that takes a long time to play out – consider how long biotechnology took to change the pharma industry, or how slowly the renewable energy revolution seems to be moving.

There is an important caveat here: just because disruption happens slowly doesn't make it easy to navigate. Indeed, John's story as CEO of Pearson for eight years is one of painful adjustment to a business environment which everyone can see is shifting from print to digital, but the time it is taking to get there is uncertain and the way in which it is getting there is often spasmodic and unpredictable. We will say a lot more about this later on in Chapters 2 and 6.

Myth: Established firms are unable to adapt.

Reality: Once again, there are a few famous cases like Kodak that catch our eye, but they are very much the exceptions that prove the general rule. The reality is that most incumbent firms find successful ways of adapting, sometimes by fighting back directly and keeping new entrants at bay, sometimes by doubling down on their existing areas of strength, sometimes by diversifying into new business areas. Again, we will say a lot more about these and other strategies in the next few chapters.

In sum, we would say the established narrative of unicorns and dinosaurs is wrong. Staying with animal metaphors, incumbents are more like the mythical phoenix that rises from the ashes, or (with apologies to former IBM CEO Lou Gerstner), they are like elephants that have learnt to dance.[2]

Data on the amount of disruption in the economy is important for several reasons. Understanding the reality of the past makes us better prepared for the future. For example, many observers claim we are on the cusp of full-scale disruption in industries such as finance, insurance and education. This analysis reminds us that people have been making these same predictions – erroneously – since the 1990s. Knowing why these industries have not been significantly disrupted so far helps us to predict how things might actually play out over the next few years.

Better analysis also helps executives make better decisions. It's often argued that the only way to fight a tech disruptor is to beat it at its own game, for example by creating a new business in a separate unit. But we have found there are at least three other valid strategies a company might want to adopt, depending on the circumstances, as we discuss later on in Chapter 3. Companies that approach competitive threats soberly and systematically will make smarter choices about how to adapt to today's digital world.

CHANGES IN THE FORTUNE 500

Here is the data in Julian's *Harvard Business Review* article. (Note that this data examines the shift from 1995 to 2020, when the number of new arrivals on the Fortune 500 was only 17. In the main text we have updated the analysis to note that there are now 24 companies who were formed in 1995 or later.)

Consider first the Fortune 500 in 2020. Of that list, 17 were new, while 483 had existed in some form or other since before 1995. You can also look at the data the other way round and ask how many of the Fortune 500 from 25 years ago have actually gone bankrupt?

The answer is 35 – the other 465 are either still going today or have been bought out (usually for a good price) by a competitor or private equity buyer. When you look at the Global 500, the picture is similar. Only 12 of the companies included today did not exist in 1995 and only 10 of the firms included back then have since gone bankrupt. While 150 companies have dropped off the Global 500, 164 held their spots and 324 already existed in 1995.

DETAILED ANALYSIS

The figure below shows what has happened to the firms on the 1995 lists and where those on the 2020 lists came from. In the US list, 198 of the top 500 firms in 1995 were still there in 2020. A further 256 dropped off the list because they were sold to other big firms or private equity, or they simply stopped growing. Only 35 of that group died (defined as shareholders losing their money). Looking in more detail at 2020, 231 were firms that existed back in 1995 and grew sufficiently to get promoted onto the list, 54 were spinouts and restructurings of existing businesses, and only 17 were genuinely new (Facebook, Google, Tesla, Netflix, Uber etc.).

CHANGES IN THE FORTUNE 500 BETWEEN 1995 AND 2020

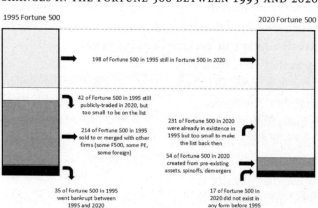

We did the equivalent analysis on the Global 500. Looking at the 1995 list, 164 of these companies were still there 25 years later, 10 died, 150 dropped off the list and 132 were sold. The 2020 list includes only 12 entirely new companies and 324 that are new to the list but made up of previously existing companies. The big change here is geopolitical: 95 fewer companies from Japan on the Global 500 in 2020 and 116 more from China compared to 1995.

The bottom line: there has been less creative destruction than prior studies have suggested and indeed less than most people believe.

There are several caveats and qualifiers. Some people ask about the make-up of the sample – no private/venture backed firms or professional partnerships, only a 25-year period of time. These are indeed limitations, but relaxing these constraints doesn't discredit the basic findings.

A bigger concern is that the Fortune 500 is based on sales revenues not market value or profitability. We didn't use the former because valuation is merely the current sentiment in the market about a firm's future growth potential – which, at the moment, would reflect the dominant narrative of digital disruption that we are challenging. Meanwhile, a dive into the profitability of firms that have stayed on the list show that, while there are anecdotal examples of margins being squeezed due to digital disruption in certain industries, most are as profitable today as they were back then.

Here is a more detailed analysis of changes in growth and profitability. The figure below breaks firms out into five categories and shows their revenue changes over the last 25 years. *Mainstays* are the 198 firms in both lists. *Fallers* are firms on the 1995 list that were either sold or stopped growing. *Risers* are firms on the 2020 list that already existed in some shape or form in 1995. *Doomed* are the 35 from the 1995 list that went bankrupt. *New Arrivals* are the 17 mostly digital firms that have been created since 1995.

The New Arrivals are of course growing rapidly, but equally impressive is the continued growth of the Mainstays. Even the Fallers – who fell out of the Fortune 500 at some point – still show some growth.

We don't show the data on profitability here (it is available in Julian's 2022 *Harvard Business Review* article), but it is a similar story with the New Arrivals starting out unprofitable but now with very large profits and the Mainstays continuing to grow their profits year after year (apart from 2008, the year of the global financial crisis). Even the Fallers' profitability has crept up over time. Only the 35 Doomed firms lost profitability.

The bottom line: yes, the big-tech New Arrivals are doing extremely well, but the incumbent Mainstays are also doing very well. There is no evidence to suggest the New Arrivals are succeeding at the expense of the old incumbents.

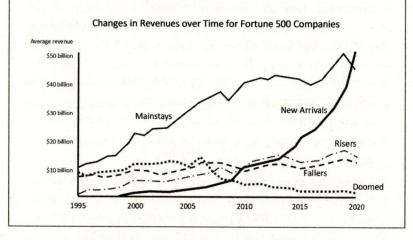

Changes in Revenues over Time for Fortune 500 Companies

A SEMI-CONTRARIAN POINT OF VIEW

So, what is this book about? We wrote it as a guide to the challenges of digital transformation in incumbent companies – and the factors that help them become resurgent. Here, we cover all the different facets of digital transformation from the technologies themselves through new digital ways of working to leadership and culture. We added a chapter at the end specifically on Generative AI, given that it is now seen to be the pre-eminent digital issue facing major companies, as well as the wider world.

The book offers a particular view borne of our own experiences, namely that incumbents are learning and adapting remarkably well. Resurgence refers to a revival or turnaround in fortune after a period of limited activity or popularity, and we think the concept captures nicely what established firms are currently going through. We like to think of it as semi-contrarian. We're not denying what's happening in the world of new technology but we see huge advantages – as well as disadvantages – in incumbency. Our intention is to provide a view grounded in evidence and theory, to help you make smart and balanced decisions, and that means not falling for the hysteria that often surrounds digital technologies. Here are some key themes and lessons that we will come back to multiple times over the course of the book.

1. *Beware the Hype.* It's an unfortunate truth that new technologies *always* get hyped up ahead of their capacity to deliver. For example, Tesla CEO Elon Musk said in 2023 that ChatGPT was the most powerful tool for creativity ever invented. Only time will tell if this is true. But remember that he also told us autonomous vehicles would be on our roads by the mid-2010s – and that didn't really work out so well.

Once in a while a new technology creates genuinely rapid changes in how we live our lives – think of the iPhone and its app store. But most others take a long time to play out, or they end up being complete duds. What this means, from a business perspective, is that you can afford to take the long view. There are risks in investing too late when a new technology comes along, but there are also risks in investing too early. And of course, you cannot control the timing of change – user adoption is a function of many factors, most of which are beyond your influence.

Our advice here is essentially to adopt a *fast second* strategy when it comes to new technology.[3] Keep a watchful eye on what's coming down the track, be piloting and experimenting but also be confident enough to let others make the big early investments and be ready to move quickly – using all the levers of influence at your disposal – when you see signs that the market is ready.

2. *Remember that digital isn't just about technology*. There are plenty of technical aspects to digital transformation and you need to make sure you have a chief technology/digital/information officer who can help you make sense of all the latest trends. But if you take the long-term perspective again, the shift from analogue to digital affects many different facets of a company.

Consider the example of the Enel Group, the most valuable energy utility in Europe, with 65,000 employees operating across 30 countries, and with more than half of its energy coming from renewable sources. Under former CEO Francesco Starace, Enel put in place a major digital transformation programme from 2015 to 2022. There were huge changes in IT activities, with a shift to the Cloud and the creation of digital hubs in each business unit. There was also a big investment in customer-facing aspects of the business, including the early adoption of smart meters, interactive bills and new subscription models. But there were also big digitally-driven changes in power generation and distribution (e.g. digital twins of plants to optimize processing, augmented reality to improve maintenance), there were experiments with new digital business models around e-mobility and smart cities, and new agile ways of working were brought in, enabled by more effective information sharing.

Digital transformation, in other words, requires you to take a holistic view of your organization and to use new technologies as a lever for making changes across all functional areas of businesses to help you maintain your competitiveness. This multifaceted approach is central to the approach we take in this book, with each chapter looking at a different part of your business.

3. *Adopt a disruptive mindset*. The most successful incumbents are the ones that develop an eye for disruption – seizing opportunities to develop new digitally-enabled products and services – while still reaping the rewards of their strong incumbent market positions. This disruptive mindset sometimes requires you to actively cannibalize your existing products (before someone else does) and it sometimes means acting more defensively. As we discuss at length in the following chapters, it is not an easy balance to achieve. In the words of the author F. Scott Fitzgerald, the test of a first-rate intelligence is the ability to hold two opposing ideas in the mind at the same time and still retain the ability to function.[4] To get the balance right, one useful maxim is *learn, don't guess*. Rather than going all-in on a new technology, there are usually ways to de-risk the investment by experimenting with a new product offering, or a new way of working, on a small scale.

While this experimental approach to change is often talked about, it is still a mode of operating that most top executives are uncomfortable with. We will share plenty of stories from Pearson and from other companies where mistakes were made by going too big too soon. If we can encourage you to learn from these errors, and to build the capacity to change in a more agile and iterative way, we will have succeeded.

4. *Make continual change seem natural and familiar.* In his final email to Pearson colleagues when he retired from the company in 2020, John quoted Bob Dylan: he (or she) not busy being born is a busy dying. Pearson had been busy being born for 175 years, he wrote, and long may that continue. The point being that change is constant, it's a natural state, and the best way of thinking about any transition you go through is that the 'new' organization will itself be a transient form that sooner or later a future leader will want to change.

A key feature of this book is our emphasis on *leading* the process of digital transformation. We address the technical and strategic challenges in depth but in addition, we focus a lot on the personal challenges the leader faces and the difficulties he or she faces in enabling attitude and behavioural change among employees.

A big part of leading change well is getting the narrative right. Describing change in grand, sweeping, industry disrupting terms – which many CEOs like to do – can be deeply disempowering for people in the company, especially the middle managers, to whom most of your employees look for their daily guidance. Change is disempowering when it seems large, vague and far away; it can be empowering when the change seems small, specific and near term. So, a change programme needs an overall narrative – the light on the hill that colleagues can aspire to – but it also needs to be broken into as many small, specific, practical actions as possible.

It also really helps to be as open and honest as possible – and to really listen to colleagues at all levels of the company as they describe the fears and frustrations that large-scale change inevitably bring in its wake. You can't back off from changes that have to be made, but being open and accepting of what's not working in the process and engaging with the detail goes a long way towards keeping people with you.

5. Incumbents will (almost) always find a way. There are a few well-known cases of incumbents that have failed. Some were hit by seismic changes to their industries (Kodak and Polaroid); some made huge risky blunders (Silicon Valley Bank, Lehman Brothers) and some were overleveraged when the market turned against them (Toys 'R' Us, Thomas Cook). But these are genuinely exceptional cases. In the vast majority of incumbent companies, executives are smart enough to steer a course through, even when the risks are existential.

Nokia is an extreme case in point. Sure, the Nokia handsets business became worthless within three years of the launch of the iPhone. And, while on the eve of the launch of the iPhone, the market capitalization of Apple and Nokia was broadly similar (at around $110 billion), Apple is now (as we write this) worth 170 times more than Nokia, at almost $3.5 trillion. But 100 years ago the Nokia Corporation was into forestry and rubber boots, and a few other things besides. It reinvented itself several times over the intervening period. When it sold its handsets business to Microsoft in 2014, it shifted its attention back to the mobile infrastructure (networks) business, buying out its joint venture partner Siemens and merging with Alcatel-Lucent Enterprise. Today, Nokia is a successful and growing technology company, market leader in its field, with some 90,000 employees in 130 countries around the world. So, even in the extremely rare case where a company is disrupted as catastrophically as Nokia was, there is still a chance to survive and find your way through.

This is an important theme, and not just because most of the people reading this book are likely to be working in incumbent companies and want to be reassured. It's important because people often draw false analogies from failure. At some point, you have probably heard a colleague warn 'this could be our Kodak moment' as a spur for investing in something new and unproven. Our view is, fine, consider how your situation might be like Kodak's. But as well as worrying about the advantages the nimble startups have going for them as they seek to disrupt you, you should also keep track of your substantial advantages as an established competitor – a well-known brand, loyal customers, deep pockets, approval from regulators and deep capabilities in important areas. These are important aspects of the incumbent's advantage.

BOOK STRUCTURE

Consistent with our view that digital isn't just about technology, we cover a wide range of topics in this book, with each chapter homing in on one key challenge or issue:

Chapter 1. The essence of digital transformation: Fixing the engine while flying the plane. Incumbent companies aren't just trying to figure out the new digital technology, they are trying to keep the old technology going as well. This 'ambidextrous' way of working requires great skill and here we share a few thoughts on how to get it right.

Chapter 2. Timing and pacing: How and When to respond to new technologies. You don't want to be late to market, but you don't want to be too early either. This chapter provides examples from many industries, with advice on when to act and also what tactics you should adopt when you do so.

Chapter 3. Digital business models: New ways to make money. There is a lot of talk about platforms and ecosystems in the business world today. Here, we discuss the various ways that digital technology is enabling new business models and we offer a framework to help you think about new options for your own company.

Chapter 4. Digital ways of working: From agile to virtual. One of the less well-understood consequences of digital technology is that it allows organizations to operate on a much flatter and less hierarchical basis than before. This in turn allows new ways of working, such as the well-known agile methodology. Here, we address the different implications of digital technology for your internal structures and processes.

Chapter 5. Investing in digital infrastructure: A non-technical guide. This isn't the book to read if you want a technical guide to Cloud computing, cybersecurity or digital marketing. But if you want to know *how* you should think about the adoption of these technologies, we have some useful advice. This chapter is strictly for the non-techies who need to work effectively with the engineers.

Chapter 6. Leading change: The people and cultural challenge. Ultimately, digital transformation requires good leadership – it needs strong internal leadership in terms of giving people a sense of what needs to be done when and it needs strong external leadership to keep other stakeholders on board. Here, we also talk about what we mean by a 'digital mindset' and how we can nurture it more effectively.

Chapter 7. How might ChatGPT change the world? This final chapter takes a close look at Generative AI, with a short discussion of how it works, then a longer discussion of its implications for individual productivity, for how companies operate and for society more broadly. As with all new technologies, Generative AI has been somewhat overhyped, so we seek to offer a balanced perspective here.

Afterword. A short final personal reflection from John on leading a company through digital disruption.

A note on the 'voice' used in this book. The book is a mix of John's personal reflections, Julian's experiences as a consultant and professor, and the discussions that the two of us have had over the last three years. We have used a mixture of third-person narrative, where we refer to John or Julian's specific story, and first-person plural to discuss our generalized point of view about what readers need to do. However, there are a few anecdotes that are sufficiently personal to John so we have left them in the first-person singular – they can be easily identified because we have used a small indent and italicized the text in question.

WHO IS THE BOOK FOR?

This book is designed for businesspeople. People who are in full-time jobs, who are working in companies that are going through some form of digital transformation. They may be mid-change or they might just be starting out. And it is written for people who are in mid to senior positions, individuals who have some responsibility for thinking strategically about the future and understanding both the opportunities and challenges of digitization.

It should also be of interest to consultants and advisors, and to students studying the topic of digital transformation. We don't get much into the underlying theory but there is sufficient referencing at the back (*see* page 201) to guide you if you want to do some further reading.

In sum, we anticipate three main learning outcomes from this book:

Awareness – Understanding what is happening in the business world today and contemporary examples of companies who have successfully and not successfully made the analogue to digital transition. Through this you will also understand the vernacular and the buzzwords of today so that you can have smarter conversations with your colleagues.

Big Ideas – Understanding the main concepts and frameworks that will help you make better decisions. Some of these ideas came from other academics and practitioners. Some are our own, building on articles we have published in leading journals in recent years.

Practical Advice – What you can do differently? There are two aspects to this. One is how do you make the Big Bets? How do you make the right decisions around investing in some of these technologies? But we also have advice on a more micro level, what might you do differently on Monday morning? We want to give you practical ideas of the tools and the techniques that you can use in your day-to-day work with your immediate colleagues.

1

The Essence of Digital Transformation

In July 2019, John announced the death of the college textbook. It was a big moment in the publishing industry and attracted due levels of media attention. 'Pearson accelerates push to digital first publishing,' announced the *Financial Times* (*FT*).[1] Savings to students 'to the tune of more than $600m' were predicted by one American news outlet.[2] Another anticipated a 'scrum for survival'[3] as the textbook industry moved away from printed books. However, as is often the case, what seems like a big strategic move was in fact a series of small steps that culminated in a moment that had been years in the making. Here is John's account of what transpired.

I declared that Pearson would move from a text-based edition-led cycle every three years to a digital first model with insight and event-driven content and technology updates, integrated with personalized feedback. For example, there had been 17 editions of Philip Kotler's bestselling Principles of Marketing *textbook with a new edition published at least every three years since 1980. There would be no 18th edition. Instead, the digital courseware would be continuously updated with professors and students always accessing the latest edition, which would never be out of date. By integrating content and assessment, Pearson could provide continuous feedback to students and their teachers. This data-driven guidance would help students better absorb course material and master difficult concepts. They*

1

would be able to listen to the content as they travelled to college or worked out in the gym and they could still obtain a physical copy or download and print it if needed.

As well as a big change in the product, this was a radical shift in Pearson's business model. Rather than students buying and owning a physical textbook, which retailed for up to $300, they would pay much less – as little as $40 to access digital courseware for the duration of their studies. This represented a dramatic shift in the economics of the publishing industry and highlighted the huge change in the market.

Why did we decide that 2019 was the right time to make the difficult and, in the short term, financially challenging shift from paper to digital textbooks? A major factor was that over the prior five years, industry revenues had declined by 40 per cent in real terms as students had moved rapidly from owning physical textbooks to renting them.

This shift, in turn, had been enabled by the growth of Amazon and other e-commerce platforms. We saw what had happened to the music industry and their experience with illegal downloads and subsequent shifts in consumer behaviour. We understood not to waste time fighting the new ways our customers wanted to engage with us but rather to move as swiftly as possible to embrace digital access and, in the process, abandon our attachment to our belief that customers continued to want physical ownership. It was, in essence, a fight for survival.

This shift enabled us to tackle an existential threat. When CNN Money published a feature on America's biggest rip-offs,[4] college textbooks featured prominently alongside movie theatre popcorn, hotel mini bars and wine in restaurants. Since that first edition of Philip Kotler's marketing textbook had been published in the 1970s, textbook prices had increased by over 1,000 per cent, three times the rate of inflation. It was not surprising, therefore, that when enabled by the emergence of digital platforms, the secondary market for college textbooks scaled quickly, causing huge financial damage to publishers.

For all the short-term financial pain, the longer-term shift to an access model will ultimately be financially beneficial for Pearson and its competitors. There is no second-hand market in e-books, *so demand is much more predictable. The costs of production are dramatically lower as there is very little printing. Online sales bring more predictable revenues, greater visibility on performance and higher-quality earnings, all of which are viewed highly favourably by shareholders as well.*

For the product, this was the vision we'd been driving to for more than a decade – content plus assessment powered by technology, delivering personalized learning at scale. With the digital platform built, it then becomes much easier to continually innovate and add new features – as Pearson is now doing by creating new AI-inspired learning tools that provide individualized support, practice and feedback tailored to meet the needs of every learner.

For the business model, the growth of the secondary market brought the growing realization that shifting from an ownership to an access model was not just a case of do or die for the company, but in time would make a better business. The timing, crucially, was right too. By 2019, we had re-platformed the company to be truly digital and mobile first, enabling us to reduce the cost base significantly so that we could be profitable at a much lower price point.

We had aligned colleagues, authors and industry partners around the vision and all the detailed changes that it required. Crucially, customers were ready for it too. Many students now preferred an e-book to a printed textbook, although a substantial minority continue to prefer a print version, which meant we expected the pace of the analogue to digital transition to continue to be messy and uneven for some years to come.

How did this big strategic change play out? Pearson had been going through a tough time for several years at this point. From 2014 to 2019, the value of US college publishing revenues had declined 40 per cent in real terms. And importantly, all the main competitors were struggling. Cengage went into Chapter 11 bankruptcy in 2013, McGraw-Hill Education was taken into private ownership the same year, amid heavy losses. There was no easy way through this challenging set of circumstances.

Ultimately, Pearson's commitment to 'digital first' in college textbooks in 2019 was a turning point.[5] The company is now fully focused on educational publishing as a digital service and, after a decade of industry-wide decline, revenues are set to grow again.

DIGITAL TRANSFORMATION – TWO DIFFERENT ASPECTS

The story of Pearson's digital transition – with the death of the college textbook as the symbolic turning point – is what this book is all about. It is the story of a very successful incumbent, the biggest most profitable college textbook publisher in the world, pondering how best to respond to the threat of digital disruption. As digital technology becomes better, cheaper and more pervasive, there is a huge imperative for incumbents to adapt – in two distinct ways.

One aspect of this adaptation is internal and mostly behind-the-scenes. In the case of Pearson, this included shifting from traditional analogue printing to digital software, building new IT systems and rethinking aspects of how thousands of individuals do their job. Pearson – like most companies – invested a huge amount of time and money into these types of improvements.

The other aspect of this adaptation is external and visible to all. For Pearson it boiled down to a simple question: at what point should the printing press be turned off? When do we explicitly state to our market, our students and universities, that from now on college texts will be primarily digital rather than paper-based books? It's a difficult decision for incumbents to make, as we will discuss below, because it means killing off your existing source of earnings in the hope of creating a new one. The fable of Kodak's demise reminds us of what can happen if you get this decision wrong.

How generalizable is Pearson's experience? The college textbook industry has obvious and important similarities to newspapers, music, books, television, movies and photography. These are industries that create digital content – information and entertainment – that has no need to ever exist in a physical form. Companies in these industries create and distribute intellectual property mostly in the form of bits and bytes. Their development costs are high, but the marginal cost of selling their products to additional customers is close to zero. In all such cases, the challenge of transitioning from 'analogue to digital' is existential for the incumbents. We will have a lot more to say about such companies in the next chapter on timing and pacing.

In other industries, the threat of digital disruption is generally not as severe. Sure, digital technology has a dramatic effect on *how* we purchase things but, ultimately, there is still a physical product or a tangible service. We still want to buy food, clothes, houses, refrigerators and cars. We still want to go on holiday, go out with our friends and get our hair cut. We want to stay healthy, we need access to money and so on. But even if digital disruption isn't an existential threat to these types of product and service companies, there are still some difficult choices facing incumbents. Consider the automobile industry. Tesla and BYD are single-mindedly focused on creating digitally enabled electric vehicles and their strategic challenge is simply one of pushing their chosen business model as far and as fast as they can. Everything is aligned around that common goal.

But Volkswagen, Toyota and GM have a more complicated calculation to make. They are investing in digital/electric vehicles because that's where the market growth is, but they also have existing customers to serve and profits to defend in the old world of internal combustion engine vehicles. They are riding two horses. They are fixing the engine while flying the plane. Which in turn creates big tensions for them internally as they figure out how – and how quickly – to shift resources from the old technology to the new one.

Here's how Gavin Patterson, former CEO of BT Group and Chief Revenue Officer of Salesforce, framed the dilemma when we interviewed him:

Starting as CEO in 2013, I was faced with a very real threat early on in my tenure. We had a highly profitable business generating decent cash flow, but it was declining in revenues, declining in average revenue per user (ARPU) and heavily regulated. If we didn't move into new markets quickly, then over a 10- to 20-year period, the business would likely die.

At the same time, I was under pressure from the board to deliver results quarter to quarter and so I was faced with a very real dilemma. How to keep the existing business going whilst finding and bringing onboard new revenue streams?

This is an important theme throughout this book and it serves us all well to underline the point. Digital *transformation* is the ongoing process of moving into a world where almost everything has a digital element to it. Every company has to work on this challenge. Digital *disruption* is a much narrower concept – it is a specific set of circumstances whereby incumbents try to steer a narrow course between growing a new area of business and protecting an existing one.

The remainder of this chapter focuses on digital disruption, in terms of why it happens and what you can do about it.

WHAT DO WE MEAN BY DISRUPTION?

The theory of disruption is associated with the late Clayton Christensen, a professor at Harvard Business School. Christensen became legendary within the world of academia for his research, looking at the evolution of the disk-drive industry in personal computers.[6] He showed that as every generation of disc got smaller and smaller, a new company every time would become the market leader. In other words, even though an incumbent with a larger disc wanted to make the transition to a slightly smaller disc, they failed in that shift. He came up with a theory of why this disruption happens – why incumbents miss out on the new opportunity even though they are trying to capture it.

The classic example is Kodak – why did they miss the shift to digital imaging? Did they fail to invest in the new technology? No – in fact, Kodak invented the digital camera in 1975 and put billions of dollars into digital technologies. Did they fail to listen to their customers? No again. Instead, they listened too carefully to the wrong customers. At the time when digital imaging was first taking off, Kodak was doing a really good job of selling high-quality film to its most sophisticated customers – for example, professional photographers.

All through the 1990s, as digital cameras were first emerging as low-end products, Kodak was aware that a shift was happening. It was putting some investment into that emerging market space. But most of Kodak's energy was spent trying to sell ever higher-quality traditional film to its most sophisticated customers. As they were doing that, digital cameras were evolving to become considerably higher-quality. Digital cameras were on a trajectory of rapid improvement from the low end of the market to the mid-market. At some point, in the early 2000s, those digital cameras became good enough quality to capture the interests of the mainstream market that Kodak was trying to serve. That's when the alarm bells started to go off.

Now, Kodak could see that this was happening, but because they had focused mostly on their higher-end customers, and because their existing products were so profitable, they had not devoted enough resources to build the necessary capabilities in digital cameras. By the time they figured out that digital cameras were a genuine threat, it was too late. The alternative providers who were coming through with digital cameras were far better placed than Kodak and more focused on making it work. Kodak scrambled to adapt but they never recovered. They were never able to reposition their business model, which had been focused on more traditional film and cameras rather than the new realities of the digital market. That in a nutshell is the theory of disruption. And, of course, standalone digital cameras themselves didn't last long, with the advent of the everything-in-one smartphone.

Christensen framed the challenge facing Kodak's executives as 'The Innovator's Dilemma'. At the point in time when action is clearly needed, the time when such action might be effective has passed. Therefore, to avoid this particular dilemma, we must learn how to take anticipatory action – we need to act at a point when the way forward is *not* clear.

DIFFERENT TECHNOLOGIES, DIFFERENT TRAJECTORIES

The concept of disruption is now well established. Most senior executives are familiar with the concept and of course they are worried by it. It is a worrying phenomenon because if you get it wrong, you run the risk that your business goes the way of Kodak or Blockbuster Video, the retail video rental company that failed to anticipate the shift to streaming services and went bankrupt in 2010. It is also a fascinating concept to people because in some ways it is completely inevitable. It is not a story about executives stupidly missing the market but rather, a story about executives making what seem like sensible decisions all the way and these sensible decisions lead them down the wrong path. But the reality of disruption is a little bit more nuanced – and a little less scary – than this theory might suggest. There are two important points to make.

First, the situation where a new technology *completely* replaces an old technology is not that common. Business schools are a case in point. Ten years ago, many observers said we would be disrupted by online learning, as it had all the hallmarks of a disruptive technology. Online offerings grew rapidly, but as people experimented, it became clear there were significant limitations to learning online as well as huge benefits. During Covid we all made the shift online through necessity, but post-Covid, we moved largely back to in-person teaching.

Using the earlier theory of disruption, we see that online learning started out as a low-quality offering. It improved as we moved through the 2000s and the ability to create online courses increased. But then the quality of that offering plateaued. Unlike digital imaging, which followed a steady upward trajectory, the performance trajectory of online learning was steep at first and then it plateaued.

TWO DIFFERENT TRAJECTORIES OF DEVELOPMENT FOR
A NEW TECHNOLOGY

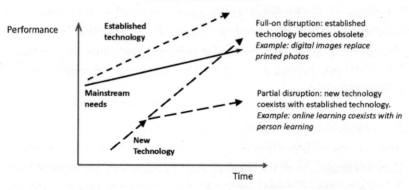

There are, in other words, two possible endpoints. One is that the new technology becomes good enough for adoption by the mainstream market and therefore renders the old technology obsolete. The other is that the new technology matures to a point that it is attractive to one segment of the market but not others, allowing it to coexist with the old technology. Online learning seems destined to exist alongside in-person learning for the foreseeable future. In trade publishing, e-books will coexist with paper books. Online shopping will continue to coexist with retail shopping. Streaming movies online at home coexists with going to see a movie in a cinema or movie theatre.

The second point to make about the threat of disruption is that incumbents have a range of different tactics available to them in response. We will say a lot more about this in the next chapter but suffice it, for now, to say that 'fighting back' directly against a low-end emerging competitor isn't always the right way forward. The vast majority of incumbents find some path to survival, even when faced with a really disruptive technology. Kodak and Blockbuster are the exceptions, not the rule. One powerful tactic is diversification. One might argue that it was a failure of imagination on Kodak's part not to see how it could adapt its core capabilities and technologies to meet the needs of new and growing markets. Its major competitor, Fujifilm, diversified – adapting its existing in-house technologies to meet the needs of future markets – and did much better than Kodak as a result. Likewise, while in this book we focus a lot on the challenges Pearson faced in the digital transformation of its college publishing business, the company's diversification into adjacent markets – applying its expertise to grow in areas like professional certification, assessment, language learning, work-based learning and virtual schooling – has been crucial to its survival and subsequent resurgence.

YOUR DIGITAL DISRUPTION PLAYBOOK

There is no simple formula for incumbents when facing digital disruption. We are happy to share our experience and offer advice, but every industry has its own dynamic and its own special circumstances. The more examples you have to play with, the more likely you are to come up with the right course of action for your own industry. But even though we cannot tell you what to do, we can help you figure out the relevant dimensions of the puzzle. In our experience, there are three interlocking elements:

- Structure – what is the right organizing model for addressing a disruptive threat?
- Mindset – how should you and your colleagues think about the disruptive threat?
- Identity – how does this disruptive threat affect your company's purpose?

Of course, there are plenty of other things to think about – for example, the expectations of your multiple stakeholders, the skills and capabilities you need to be successful, the reactions of competitors and so on. But we see these three as the most consequential, the most likely to determine your ultimate success or failure. We will take each one in turn.

Structure – Separation or Integration?
Consider a successful case of digital transformation – *Autotrader*. Through the 1980s and 1990s in the UK, *Autotrader* was the magazine-of-choice if you wanted to buy or sell a used car. With the advent of the internet in the mid-1990s, *Autotrader* could easily have lost out to an entrepreneurial startup like Craigslist or eBay, but its executive team responded quickly, Catherine Faiers, the current chief operating officer, recalled:

> *The first thing the team did well [in the late 1990s] was to define the threat, then immediately try and find the opportunity in that threat. That's always the art – if you can figure out how to bring your strengths to the table, you are likely to be successful.*

The decision was taken to create a separate online sales unit in London (several hours' drive from the Manchester HQ) and to give it a licence to cannibalize the existing print-based business. The online unit reported directly to the CEO. As Catherine recalled:

> *They took all the existing infrastructure, almost ring-fencing it, and said, you keep doing what you're doing here – you keep publishing the magazine each week, getting local dealers and people to advertise their cars in it. [Meanwhile] let's get the specialist unit of people focused on technology and the website and get them going to market with a separate digital proposition.*

This structure allowed the digital business to grow quickly. The online business got 'all sorts of unfair advantages' that a digital startup would never have had, including the brand, data on existing customers and access to the parent company's financial and human resources. *Autotrader* quickly became the online car marketplace of choice. The print-based business was closed down in the early 2010s. Since then, *Autotrader*, as a wholly-digital business, has gone from strength to strength.

While the means of implementing this print-to-digital transformation seems obvious, *Autotrader* still stands out as an unusual case because of the aggressive cannibalization engineered by the leadership team at the time. As Catherine said:

> *Of all the digital transformations I've seen, it was probably the most extreme example in terms of how much risk they were prepared to put their core business under to achieve the desired future state.*

The heart of *Autotrader*'s successful transition was separation – a new unit set up far from head office, free to do whatever it took to succeed and with the CEO's explicit backing. This is indeed the standard model for coping with a disruptive change, an approach advocated in Clayton Christensen's original book in 1997[7]. But as ever, the story is a little more nuanced than that. Complete separation was the correct tactic for *Autotrader*, but there are other situations where greater connectedness is needed.

Consider the Swedish industrial company, Sandvik.[8] It makes heavy-duty mining equipment, digging machines and such like. But digitalization has also come to the mining industry, so Sandvik invests heavily in sensors and monitoring equipment on its machinery, to optimize how it is used and thus make the whole process of mining more efficient.

The original digital team at Sandvik was a team embedded tightly within their services division, which provided services to their various customers around the world. They experimented with how to digitize their service offering, with many trial-and-error iterations. There was such deep interlinkage between the digital services they were building and the actual equipment they were using that a fully integrated mode of operation was entirely necessary.

By 2012, they realized that they had created a digitally-enabled service offering, which they called *My Sandvik,* and it was gradually rolled out to customers, not just for Sandvik mining equipment, but for all their customers' other equipment as well, including from Sandvik's competitors. As My Sandvik emerged as a commercial product, the team was spun out into a separate business unit, increasingly operating at arm's-length from the Sandvik service division they had started in. This gave them the freedom to work with third parties and create application programme interfaces (APIs) to interact with other companies' equipment.

Sandvik's solution to the digital transformation challenge, in other words, was the opposite of *Autotrader's. Autotrader* created a separate unit which was gradually integrated back into the rest of the organization as that unit's sales took off. Sandvik started out with an embedded unit, which was gradually given more freedom over time, the more successful it became.

So, given the different models chosen by *Autotrader* and Sandvik, both successful in their own right, how should you make your own choice? Here's a simple framework developed by our colleague, Costas Markides.[9]

On the vertical dimension, you have the level of conflict between the new activity and your existing activities. Conflict essentially means the potential for the new activity to cannibalize the sales of the existing activity. In a conflict there are winners and losers so that situation needs to be handled with great care.

On the horizontal dimension, you have the relatedness of the assets required to make the digital business work. For example, consider the brand, the distribution and sales team, the manufacturing capacity, the underlying technology, the support activities and so on, and for each one, ask yourself how important the company's existing assets are to the success of the new digital business.

FOUR OPTIONS FOR BUILDING A NEW BUSINESS ALONGSIDE AN EXISTING ONE

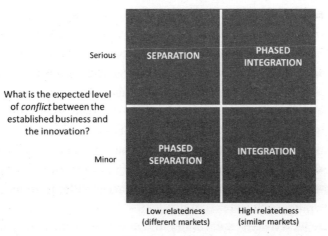

This framing suggests four generic situations and we have already discussed two of them. *Autotrader* was a case that required 'phased integration'. There was high conflict between the new and the old parts, but also a high level of relatedness in their activities. The online business was initially kept separate and then integrated over time as it became a success.

Sandvik was the opposite. It started as an integrated activity because it was so tightly embedded and required operational linkages with the mainstream activities. However, as it gradually became a worthwhile business and evolved into a software product, it became clear that there was an opportunity to grow it, to actually move it into a separate division as its relatedness diminished and the product became more sophisticated and more developed. That's essentially what is termed 'phased separation'.

Now consider the other two positions in the matrix. A top-left example is Nespresso. It started out within Nestlé some 40 years ago. It was a good idea that nobody really understood at the time because Nespresso was selling a machine that made fresh coffee, in direct competition to Nestlé's existing products such as Nescafé powdered coffee. Nespresso was considered an oddity. Yes, there was some brand resonance, but in terms of how the coffee was made, the market it was serving and so forth, it conflicted with the mainstream business. It did not have huge linkages back to the existing activities. For example, Nespresso is sold in stand-alone retail shops, completely separate from the way that Nestlé sells every other product in its portfolio. It is a classic separation story. They managed to make Nespresso work, and at some point, it was spun out as a completely autonomous business unit. It now makes over a billion dollars a year of revenue on its own. Although owned by Nestlé, it is in every respect run as a separate business.

Bottom right, we have in mind a large tier-one automotive supplier selling subsystems into Volkswagen, Renault and the like. It has become quite sophisticated in using artificial intelligence (AI) to help optimize its activities, save money and make better-quality parts. AI is sufficiently new and challenging to this company that you might imagine them operating it through a separate unit but it doesn't present any internal conflicts and is only useful when properly applied to manufacturing and engineering problems so fully integrated is the way to go.

As you think about engaging in activities that are potentially disruptive, this matrix will help you figure out what the right structural arrangement might be. Bear in mind that where you start in terms of separation or integration may not be where you end up. You must be prepared to shift your structure over time, recognizing that tensions and interdependencies will evolve, as will the markets in which you are operating.

Mindset – Balancing Two Opposing Views

As we noted in the introduction to this book, the test of a first-rate intelligence – the ability to hold two opposing ideas in your mind at the same time and still retain the ability to function – is also a great definition of a disruptive mindset.

On the one hand, it is valuable to imagine a disruptive threat in everything that is going on around you. This doesn't come naturally. For example, when facing a shortfall in sales, the initial instinct of every corporate being is to talk about cyclical challenges or exceptional circumstances and to anticipate that things will go 'back to normal' soon. Your job is to push against this default behaviour – you should continually challenge the long-held beliefs and institutional biases that underplay the risk of disruption.

For example, when Pearson's US college publishing revenues first started to decline in the early 2010s, the leadership team were much more inclined to blame a decline in college enrolments, rather than accept that their pricing strategy was causing major problems and the secondary market had now become a serious competitor. It took several years before they came to accept that there was an insidious trend – technology-enabled price deflation – underway that would require drastic changes.

On the other hand, not everything that has the potential to be disruptive will turn out to be so. Five years ago, blockchain (the technology that Bitcoin is built on) was the next big thing, now not so much. Quantum Computing, we are told, is just a few years away from being commercially viable. But we were also told this 20 years ago.

There are times, in other words, when you need to be careful not to overreact. For example, in the summer of 2012, Pearson made a $150 million bet to buy the emerging leader in self-publishing, as the leaders of Penguin considered it a major disruptive threat. They were worried it would enable writers and distribution channels to disintermediate the publisher. But things didn't play out as predicted. While self-publishing has found its place in the market, it has so far failed to have much impact on major trade publishers. Pearson ended up writing off a big chunk of the purchase price. As Coram Williams, CFO of Penguin at the time the acquisition was made, reflects:

> I think our analysis of the risk from self-publishing was correct, but we didn't fully understand or place as much value on the strengths of the incumbent in the way that disruption would play out. The place of the traditional publisher even in a fully digital publishing ecosystem was still a powerful one.

Similarly, executives at the *Financial Times* – owned at the time by Pearson – were constantly worrying about the threat from well-funded disruptive new entrants like the *Huffington Post*, *BuzzFeed* and *Business Insider*, who were taking some of their talent and looked likely to eat the *FT*'s advertising lunch. Again, these companies have found their place in the ecosystem, but they exist alongside the *FT*, *The New York Times* and the *Wall Street Journal*, rather than seriously disrupting them. That is not to say Penguin, the *FT* and others are not facing digital disruption. Publishers are increasingly dependent on one powerful distributor, Amazon, which has caused more bricks-and-mortar retailers to close than any other form of disruption. News access online has also meant that sales of print newspapers have plummeted, destroying previously highly lucrative print advertising models.

Or consider online learning again. Pearson was correct to say that MOOCs (Massive Open Online Courses) posed no direct threat to its US college publishing businesses. Course completion rates on MOOCs remain pitifully low. But companies like Coursera have built a powerful digital platform and developed an ecosystem of institutions and learners. These companies both compete and partner with Pearson in the wider ecosystem, but do not directly threaten its very existence.

Sometimes you need to act immediately and other times it pays to wait and see. You need to be constantly alert to what's going on around you and you will only know in retrospect what the right course of action was. The ability to run a business as it is today and may be tomorrow is vital to leaders navigating their way through a major digital disruption. This is why you need to keep thinking about the disruptive mindset.

Making sense of weak signals

We recognize that it isn't that helpful to say 'sometimes act quickly, sometimes wait and see'. So, let's try to be a bit more specific. The reality in any large company is that there are hundreds of things happening in your marketplace or your technology arena at any given time, so you need to find some way to tune in to the relevant 'weak signals' of change and decide which ones are worth amplifying and acting on.

The first point is to make sure those weak signals are finding their way from the front line to the executive suite. Every senior executive has their own way of keeping in touch with what's happening in the marketplace. As a general rule the more 'unfiltered' the data, the better. Jeremy Darroch, former CEO of Sky, the European media company best known for its sports and movies broadcasting, told us that he is always interested in the minority or lone voice in a meeting – the person with a contrarian argument:

> If there's five or six people talking about an issue and one person is an outlier, almost always that individual for good or bad has picked something up or spotted something that everybody else just hasn't seen. Really listening for the outliers is a very effective way of not allowing group-think at times of uncertainty.

Gavin Patterson, former CEO of BT Group and Chief Revenue Officer of Salesforce, offered a similar perspective:

> One of the challenges as a CEO is everything that's prepared is presented in a very filtered way. There is real value in the rawness of the data, the outlying feedback, how you are perceived in terms

of how easy it is to do business with you. You've got to find ways of keeping fresh, unfiltered feedback and insight and data.

The organization will protect you from it, thinking that you don't want to hear bad news, but in reality, you really want to hear what people think so that you can act quickly and make the changes required.

I made sure that I regularly spent time with our suppliers and our customers of all sizes, really deeply listening to what they said; to have that unfiltered outside-in view from people who I trusted.

Second, to deal with disagreement effectively, you need a strong executive team and board – people who are comfortable with ambiguity and up for a constructive confrontation. As a senior executive, you must be prepared to listen to the contrarians and to suspend your judgement. You need to use a mixture of data, analysis and gut feel, and to be decisive when need be.

Third, this in turn requires you to be highly attuned to what Andy Grove (former CEO of Intel) called *dissonant information*. This is the information that goes against the dominant view in the company, or indeed the entire industry, at the time.[10]

For example, put yourself in the shoes of a newspaper company in 2000, seeing print advertising revenue falling. You want to believe the drop is just part of the natural cycle, but if you go online, you start seeing ads popping up on websites. You persuade yourself – to avoid cognitive dissonance – that these new online ads are complementary to the print ads in your newspapers but at some point, it dawns on you that your print advertisers are moving online, never to return to the printed page.

Returning to the example at the beginning of this chapter, Pearson experienced much the same situation in college textbooks. The company had some 35 per cent of the US market, with gross margins in the 70–80 per cent range. Around 2012, sales started to falter and the executives running the business collectively sought to explain the problem in cyclical terms, caused by declining college enrolments. But the closer they looked at what customers were actually doing

– for example, buying second-hand versions through Amazon – the more it became clear there was a secular shift underway, with growing numbers of students finding ways to avoid buying new textbooks. The executive team were hearing a lot of noise – from customers, press, politicians – and they knew at that point they were on borrowed time. That's what led to John's decision to announce the death of the college textbook.

High-quality insight into actual consumer behaviour is, of course, a big part of the solution. Here is a perspective from Sky's former CEO Jeremy Darroch:

> I think why Sky was successful is we were able to look across the entire value chain of customer choice and harvest individual insights that could allow us to steer to where the consumer was going, as opposed to what the industry was talking about.
>
> In disruptive environments you have to do two things. You have to understand the real politik of the industry, but you also have to understand where consumer attitudes and behaviours are going. That sounds easy but it's actually quite a hard thing for a lot of broadcasters to do. As a Direct-to-Consumer business, Sky was well positioned to disseminate what was happening in the real world and push it back to our partners across the world.

Identity – Knowing What You Stand For
The third key part of managing digital disruption is getting a clear fix on your company identity. By way of analogy, a decade ago, John was being treated for throat cancer (he subsequently recovered). As he recalls:

> At a particularly low point, a friend of mine who was a Benedictine priest shared with me a quote from Martin Luther: crux probat omnia, which roughly translates as 'The Cross Tests'. You don't need to be remotely religious to appreciate the underlying idea. There are moments of personal crisis that strip away all the superfluous layers that we wrap around ourselves and reveal who we really are, at our

core. Times of corporate crisis such as industry disruption do the same to companies.

Pearson survived because in our moment of truth, we understood that our enduring value to customers was neither inherently analogue nor digital. That was just how it was made real and actualized. Instead, our value to society, through the telling of stories, reporting and commenting on news, and through enabling learning, remained great even if the medium of distribution changed. Amid all the maelstrom and confusion, publishers who continue to focus on doing these things better than anyone else could be confident of their enduring value.

College professors continue to adopt Pearson titles to teach their courses. Global citizens look to the FT to publish without fear or favour. Bestselling authors such as the Obamas still go to Penguin for their editorial nous, their marketing chops and their ability to pay eye-watering advances. Likewise, musicians still value all the expertise that a record company brings to bear to new releases and audiences of all ages still want to listen to the music that defines their youth – 'the soundtrack of our lives' – and to which the major music companies own the rights.

In short, incumbents survive when they retain a clear sense of identity. Their job is to understand what it is that they do that is of enduring and endearing value, and through all the confusion of disruption and change continue to burnish it and invest in it. It helps if a clear identity is accompanied by a strong sense of purpose, a fundamental belief that what the company does matters to the wider world.

In the case of Pearson, it was our purpose that 'we empower people to progress in their lives through learning' *that carried the company, its employees, its shareholders, its partners and its customers through some of its darkest days. As a breed, publishers, like journalists and college professors, are hardwired to be sceptical, even cynical about any change, which can make it doubly difficult for them to withstand a challenging industry disruption. But if you can convince them that you are staying true to the wider sense of purpose to the mission and that a digital transformation will enable their vital work to reach a wider audience, they will stick with you through the rough and the tumble, the restructurings and the profit warnings that change of this scale almost inevitably brings in its wake.*

THREE LEVELS OF DISTINCTIVENESS – THE CASE OF APPLE

What do we mean by identity and distinctiveness? We have an intuitive sense that companies like Apple, IKEA or Google have something unique about them and it's useful to break this concept down to three levels of analysis. First is distinctiveness at the level of activities – the products and services the company sells and how they behave in the market. Second is distinctiveness at the level of capabilities – the things the company is good at. Third is distinctiveness at the level of identity or beliefs – what the company's employees believe about the business world.[11]

THREE LEVELS OF DISTINCTIVENESS

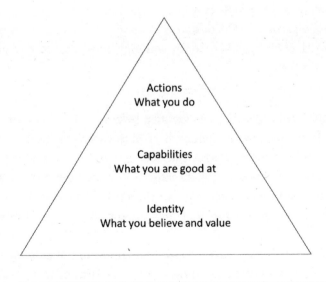

Actions
What you do

Capabilities
What you are good at

Identity
What you believe and value

Consider Apple. Everyone knows it for its products. The iPhone continues to lead, in terms of the way we think about what it is that makes a good smartphone – its functionality and its design. You can look at the iPhone and say this is what has defined Apple. However, to create the iPhone, Apple needed a set of capabilities that allowed them to create something that was completely different to what everybody else did. For example, you might say one of Apple's distinctive capabilities is a very high level of collaboration between all the different constituent parts of the business that allowed them to integrate devices whereby the hardware and the software all fit together. This collaborative capability, in turn, is made possible through an organization that does not have separate profit and loss responsibility for different divisions – everything comes together under a single profit and loss (P&L) at the level of the Chief Executive, Tim Cook.

Apple has distinctive products built through distinctive capabilities. Now, where did these capabilities come from in the first place? The answer, of course, is Steve Jobs' original vision for Apple, which was to create a company that would make 'insanely great' products which were beautifully designed and technologically sophisticated. To really understand Apple's distinctiveness, in other words, you must return to their original identity, their original purpose.

How does having a distinct identity help you in a time of digital disruption? The simple analogy here is the ship's captain in stormy seas trying to figure out which direction to go. The captain uses the North Star as it gives a clear direction of travel. Even as the weather pushes the ship off course, the North Star enables the sailors to fix that point on the horizon that they are aiming for and keep them roughly on track.

Now the challenge is that many companies do not *actually* have a clear sense of identity. Even if they did at the time of their founding, it has likely been muddied or compromised over the years. Which in turn makes it hard to codify in a way that makes sense to employees. To be clear, most companies have some sort of statement of purpose on their website, but that doesn't mean it's widely understood or believed by the company's stakeholders. But to take a more positive angle, it's useful to think through how you might define or rediscover your company's identity to help you navigate a period of digital disruption. We suggest a few key points.

First is to define your business in terms of the value you create for customers. This is sometimes called the 'job to be done'. When the handyman goes to the hardware store and says that they want to buy a drill, they do not actually want a drill, they want a hole in the wall. The drill is simply the tool and the means by which they achieve their objective – a hole in the wall. Or if you want to take the logic further, they don't want a hole in the wall, they want a picture on the wall, and they want a picture on the wall because they want a nice home.

As a company, you should therefore ask yourself: what is the job to be done? That is an effective way of elevating yourself above the here-and-now of the technology or product that you are selling. The exercise gets you to think about the value you have created for your end customers and to map that against the things you are good at (your capabilities) and your beliefs about what is important to society, regardless of whether you are in an analogue, digital or some other space. That is the means by which we think creatively about ensuring our identity is useful, sensible and practical during a time of disruption.

At Pearson, it was clear that *empowering people to progress in their lives through learning* lay at the heart of the company's identity and when John and his team were struggling with the big transition to digital this statement helped with the difficult decisions – for example, killing off the college textbook. Indeed, one of the major themes of John's tenure as CEO was a piece of work on learning efficacy, where the company sought to measure its success by focusing on the job to be done, namely students achieving their learning outcomes. We will say more about this project in Chapter 3 on digital business models.

SUMMARY OF CHAPTER

Let us pull together the key ideas from this chapter. The key point here is that successful incumbent companies face a variety of challenges from the emergence of digital technologies. Many of those challenges require significant changes – for example, root-and-branch changes to their IT infrastructure, new forms of digital marketing, or agile ways of working. There is nothing simple about any of these changes, but the 'recipe book' for making them has been well written.

But digital technology also brings with it occasional existential threats, the kind that can result in a company's entire business model being made obsolete. These are the threats we focus on in this chapter and also to some degree in the next couple of chapters. In these circumstances the 'recipe book' is vaguer, because every situation is very different and the threat level, while high, is highly variable from industry to industry.

Our solution, for want of a better term, is to keep in mind the possibility that your industry is going to be radically transformed, while also simultaneously keeping in mind the probability that in fact it will be just fine. We must keep both different mindsets operating simultaneously. We also underlined the importance of a clear sense of identity – a North Star – to provide some consistency around the difficult choices that need to be made.

In the next chapter, we consider questions of timing and pacing in more depth.

2

Timing and Pacing: How and When to Respond to New Technologies

A staple of business school education is making sense of and learning from big corporate failures – the likes of Kodak, Nokia, Blockbuster, Toys 'R' Us and BlackBerry. The reasons for these failures are complex and multifaceted, as we noted in the previous chapter. But when we ask our students, what the top executives of these companies might have done differently, the response is always 'they should have moved more quickly.'

Fair enough. Moving too slowly will often get you into trouble. However, moving too quickly is also risky. It is fraught with danger and can ultimately be very costly.

REINVENTING THE SCHOOL CURRICULUM
John learnt this lesson the hard way in 2012, during his first year as Pearson CEO. He recalls inheriting a project that was looking to create a hugely ambitious new digital curriculum for schools in America.

The project was going to 'transform the world of education' using the latest iPad-based technology from Apple and learning materials from Pearson. There was a lot of excitement about the project, inside and outside Pearson. It was going to enable the long-dreamt of vision of personalization of learning.

We had some of the most respected and most brilliant educators in America leading the project. What they were creating was exactly what national and state leaders were saying they wanted to see happen in the country's schools. We had a strong partnership with Apple and the immediate prospect of a very large contract with one of America's largest school districts. And we had already spent heavily on the project.

I reviewed the project in my first few months as CEO and worried that what we were building was far ahead of anything our customers were used to. I was sceptical that a school district would be capable of deploying a fully digital curriculum, all delivered by iPad, certainly at any sort of scale. But it would have been a very big call very early in my tenure to scrap a project that seemed to carry so much momentum and support so I quelled my reservations and we pressed ahead. Every part of the company did everything it possibly could to make the project successful. Sadly, within two years, those initial instincts proved to be well-founded. The product we created was in many ways brilliant and beautiful, but it was too comprehensive and too broad for most schools and most teachers to make full use of. The iPad also proved not to be an ideal device around which to base all learning. School technology infrastructure was nowhere near as fast or as robust as it needed to be. The consensus that previously existed between national and state leaders about the curriculum itself had broken down amidst deep political rancour. And we had problems getting the underlying platform to work consistently. The project failed and we had to write off a significant investment.

We were not the only company to make this mistake. The history of Edtech (applying new technology to education) is littered with examples of some of the world's savviest investors, like Rupert Murdoch and Bill Gates, making big investments in projects that fail to take off. It turns out that Edtech is one of the toughest industries to make progress in. Why is that? In part because the passion to invest in something that should happen – and would be truly transformational if it did – clouded some very smart people to the *fact that very often the reality is much more nuanced. To misquote T. S. Eliot, between the ideal and the reality are a lot of dark shadows.*

The other point is that education is not a B2C (business-to-consumer) market – you are not selling directly to consumers. Instead, you are working through a whole bunch of intermediaries, local school districts, state and federal regulators, and so forth, each with their own vested interests. Reforming education may not be quite as intractable a problem as reforming healthcare, but it has many of the same challenges.

So, what should we have done differently? A more iterative approach would have been much smarter. In the analogue world, publishers take their time – and spend the money necessary – to develop fully-fledged and fully-formed products before releasing to the market. They can afford to do this because they are working to a proven business model and well-trodden product development path. But in the digital world, especially when you are working with an emerging new technology or platform, product development is a more ad hoc and messier process. For example, the former CEO of The New York Times, Mark Thompson, talks about failing up to 12 times with new digital products before finding a winning formula.[1] Rather than spending tens of millions of dollars – and taking some years – to create a fully formed digital curriculum out of the box, we should have focused on launching smaller, more bite-sized digital experiences which we could get in the hands of customers earlier and learn and iterate from there. It was, in fact, a strategy that we were pursuing in other parts of the company and with a lot of success.

We will say more about this iterative approach to strategic change in the next couple of chapters. For most companies working their way through a major digital transformation, the old Facebook approach of 'moving fast and breaking things' is not the way to go. Your customers won't thank you for breaking things that they value and rely on. But 'learn, don't guess' is excellent advice – and a lesson that Pearson learnt the hard way.

LESSONS FROM OTHER INDUSTRIES

Examples of companies moving too quickly in response to new technologies are everywhere. Go back to the early 1990s when the internet first started to take off and put yourself in the shoes of the big entertainment companies – Disney, News Corporation, Time Warner. The executives heading these companies could see the internet was going to be potentially transformative to their industry because it would allow them to transmit news, music and video around the world without shipping a physical product.

So how did they respond? All three made big early bets – and all three pulled back later. For example, News Corporation run by Rupert Murdoch, bought a company called Delphi Internet Services, one of the earliest search engines, in 1993, only to sell it for a loss three years later. Disney made several big moves, acquiring Starwave (which owned ESPN.com) and 43 per cent of Infoseek, an internet service provider, and launching the GO Network, which provided access to other Disney content websites. All these assets (apart from ESPN) were shut down or sold off within a decade, with Disney taking a $800 million loss. Time Warner also moved online early, through its 1995 buyout of Turner Broadcasting and CNN.com, and then its ill-fated $165 billion merger with AOL in 2000, which was eventually unwound nine years later.

It's worth noting these mistakes aren't unique to the digital world. For example, consider the shift to renewable technologies among big oil companies. British Petroleum (BP) created a renewables strategy called 'Beyond Petroleum' in the early 2000s and spent billions of dollars trying to make it work before subsequently closing it down. In similar fashion, General Motors and Ford both created electric vehicles in the late 1990s because Californian regulators demanded they do so. They had to close those businesses down because battery technology had not developed sufficiently for mass-market use.

The point is, if you look across industry after industry, you can see the companies that got it wrong by investing too late, but you can also find examples of companies that got it wrong by investing too early. It's important to ask if this is really a problem. Does it hurt you to invest too early? The answer is it depends. Go back to Disney and their early investments in Infoseek, ABC Capital Cities and ESPN. Taken as a package, there was some real value there as well as some duds. So, Disney did not lose out by being an early investor in the internet, but if you take Time Warner merging with AOL, that was a disaster – it was one of the worst corporate deals in history and it cost the Time Warner shareholders an absolute fortune, a $99 billion write-off in 2002. Such investments don't typically lead to bankruptcy, but they can be severely bad for your health. And there is an opportunity cost, too. By focusing their time on investing early, with one big yet untested idea, these companies missed the opportunity to learn by investing incrementally in a wider range of early-stage concepts and adapting and applying what they were learning to longer-term benefit.

THE PROCESS OF TECHNOLOGICAL CHANGE

To frame this discussion on the process of technological change, we offer you two concepts – the S-Curve and the Hype Cycle.

You have surely come across the 'S-Curve' or Sigmoid Curve – it's the notion that every technology goes through a process of evolution which starts slowly, ramps up and then gradually tails off. Every S-curve is both preceded and proceeded by another S-curve, so over the long-term industrial change occurs through a series of S-curves. The computer industry is the classic example – first we had mainframe computers, then mini-computers, personal computers, laptops and now smartphones. Every generation of hardware had its own S-curve, with demand for older machines falling off (and sometimes disappearing entirely) as the new ones became popular.

There are two parts to the S-curve. There is the 'middle part' where user adoption of the technology is accelerating. For incumbent firms, the key determinant of success in this part is to make the technology as convenient and as cheap as quickly as possible. Typically called the era of *incremental change*,[2] and it is characterized by process improvements that improve quality and reduce cost. For example, the smartphone has now entered this era of incremental change, with Apple, Samsung and others making relatively small improvements to an established or 'dominant' design.

But the S-curve also has a beginning and end, with the end of one curve overlapping with the beginning of the next. This is typically called the *era of ferment* when the rules of the game are temporarily unknown and up for grabs. As everyone knows, the launch of the iPhone in 2007 led to the collapse of Nokia handsets and BlackBerry. Up to that time, most people saw the handset as a piece of hardware with increasingly sophisticated software but within a few years of the iPhone's launch, people saw the handset as an operating system-led product that gave access to a whole ecosystem of apps.

The era of ferment (2007–9 in handsets) is when incumbent companies face the greatest uncertainty. They see themselves sustaining the old S-curve for as long as possible, while also casting around for new technologies that might be emerging and deciding where to place their bets for the future.

Linking back to the previous chapter, you are likely thinking that the era of ferment is when technologies are disruptive. But it's not that simple. We do not know in advance how a given industry will evolve. The S-curve dynamic is useful to understand, but a new technology can potentially be something that creates the era of ferment, or it might be something that helps to sustain the era of incremental change.

Here is an example to make sure this is clear. Consider how the internet has affected two very different parts of the economy – the B2C (business-to-consumer) world we live in as individual users and the B2B (business-to-business) world of companies supplying products and services to each other. The internet has been highly disruptive to B2C industries, changing the way we consume news and movies and how we do our shopping. But for B2B industries – for example, companies making machinery or engineered products they sell to other companies – the internet has been a sustaining technology. Think of the 'Internet of Things' for example, the notion that we create a network of sensors that provide us with information to make the maintenance and management of our factories easier. This is a sustaining technology because it helps make incumbents stronger.

In sum, the S-curve can be decomposed into two parts – the era of incremental change and the era of ferment. When we look at digital technologies, some of those digital technologies help us through the path of incremental change, some of them are going to trigger a period of ferment and obviously the way in which we respond in each case is going to be rather different.

The second curve to throw into the mix is the Hype Cycle, popularized by Gartner,[3] the information services provider. The hype cycle is built on 'Amara's Law', named after the technologist Roy Amara. He came up with this simple notion, sometimes erroneously attributed to Bill Gates, that we tend to underestimate the long-term implications of technologies, but we overestimate their short-term implications. In other words, we jump on new technologies and we think they're going to change the world immediately, but they don't. However, in many cases they eventually do. This implies a rollercoaster cycle, with a steep upward slope towards a peak of inflated expectations quickly followed by a trough of disillusionment, then gradually leading to a slope of enlightenment and a plateau of productivity. An example is blockchain technology, which hit the peak of inflated expectations in about 2017 but by 2023 had fallen into the trough of disillusionment.

The hype cycle is a useful reminder that predictions about the power of new technologies need to be taken with a pinch of salt. At the time of writing, Generative AI is being talked about as the biggest step forward in the digital world since the internet. When you hear such statements, remember Amara's Law! Yes, Generative AI does a lot of cool stuff, but that doesn't necessarily mean it will quickly disrupt things in a profound way. The reality is that no one has yet figured out its long-term consequences, as we discuss later in Chapter 7, where we look at how ChatGPT might change the world.

The S-curve and the Hype Cycle provide complementary views on the process of technological change. It would be nice to think they provided a clear prediction for how a new technology will play out, but of course the real world is never that simple. There are uncertainties on the supply-side (i.e. how well the new technology actually works), there are uncertainties on the demand-side (i.e. how quickly users choose to adopt it) and there is plenty of room in-between for incumbents and new entrants to shape the dynamics of the evolving market to their advantage.

INSIGHTS FROM RESEARCH

In the absence of definitive statements about how new technologies play out, we can at least offer some general guidance based on a recent research paper by Julian that looked at the long-term effects of emerging technologies across six different industries.[4] The research traced the actions of the largest incumbent firms in the movie-making, newspaper, retail banking, pharmaceutical, utilities and automobile industries, when faced with potentially disruptive threats from new technologies. Here are the key findings.

First, none of the incumbents gained competitive advantage from being the early mover. Some of the early movers (for example, Time Warner merging with AOL or GM getting into electric cars in the late 1990s) got it wrong and lost a lot of money. Others (for example, the banks and newspapers that went online in the mid-1990s) did fine but were quickly followed by others so no lasting advantage was achieved by moving early. In short, the notion of first-mover advantage is overrated. A much smarter strategy is what we earlier referred to as *Fast Second*.[5] This means letting others go first, watching their moves carefully and being ready to respond quickly, if or when they start to show signs of success.

Second, all 58 of the incumbent companies survived through the 20-year period of study, despite facing major technological upheavals along the way. This may not seem like a big deal, but given all the talk about disruption, and all the references to Kodak and Nokia, it is an important data point worth keeping in mind. The fact of the matter, as we noted earlier in the introduction, is that large incumbents are pretty good at adapting to change. They usually find a way through, using a variety of different survival tactics – a point we return to in the next section.

Third, there is an important distinction between supply-side and demand-side disruption. Supply-side disruption is where the technology used to make the product changes fundamentally – consider how pharmaceutical drug development shifted from basic chemistry to biotechnology. Demand-side disruption is where the user of the product or service fundamentally changes how they behave – think about how the newspaper industry was upended by people reading their news on their tablet or smartphone.

This distinction matters because the pattern of change is quite different in the two cases. Supply-side effects are insidious. They typically play out over relatively long periods of time in a predictable way, with incumbent firms executing similar strategies though at different speeds. All the major pharmaceutical companies have now embraced biotechnology and those who were slower to do so (Pfizer, Sanofi, AstraZeneca) have not lost out significantly to those who were faster (Roche, GSK, Johnson & Johnson). Demand-side effects, by contrast, are faster-acting and more volatile, with incumbents often experimenting with a range of different business models as they seek a viable way forward in a changing market. Consider for example the contrasting ways Disney, Warner, Sony, NBC Universal and News Corporation responded to movie streaming. The box below highlights some of the tactics that are appropriate in the two cases.

The key point is simply that a better understanding of the dynamics of technological change across multiple industries should help you make better decisions for yourself. You cannot be sure how a new technology will play out, but you can look for patterns and improve the odds in your favour.

SEPARATING OUT SUPPLY-SIDE AND DEMAND-SIDE EFFECTS

As an incumbent company, a useful question to ask is where might emerging technology affect your business first? Does it operate

---

primarily on the creation of the product/service (supply side) or on the way the user consumes the product/service (demand side)?

If a *supply-side effect* is anticipated, you should respond cautiously – for example by investing small amounts in a range of different technologies, working in consortia with other firms and occasionally making acquisitions to fill gaps in expertise. Doubling down on an existing area of downstream (market-facing) expertise is likely to be helpful. Monitoring and copying the actions of competitors is often a useful defensive ploy.

If a *demand-side effect* is anticipated, there is typically more urgency to act. Building direct relationships with users, to understand how their attitudes and behaviours are changing, is important. Partnering with and/or acquiring startups through venture units or accelerators is a useful source of insight. Experimenting with new business models to explore alternative sources of revenue may be helpful. At the same time, there is also value in doubling down on existing areas of upstream expertise (such as research and development (R&D) or manufacturing) as a defensive ploy.

You should also keep an eye on the dynamics between the supply-side and demand-side. Most emerging technologies have the potential to affect firms in multiple ways and sometimes changes in one area stimulate further changes in another. In the unfortunate situation where an industry is affected simultaneously on both supply and demand sides, it is sometimes necessary to take more drastic action – for example, shifting investment into adjacent markets that are not in such a perilous position.

More broadly, and moving beyond Julian's academic research, it is generally better to focus on the big themes rather than try to predict a precise outcome when an industry is in transition.

An added complication in some industries – such as education or healthcare – is that they can be better characterized as B2B2C (business to business to consumer). In the case of college publishing, for example, the nature of the product itself is shaped by interaction with the college (does it help the professor to teach his/her course?), but how the product is consumed (do I own or rent a textbook or subscribe to get access to the digital version?) is up to the students taking the course. Pearson's big challenge in college publishing was that in the B2B part – interaction with colleges and professors – it had a high degree of visibility and change was happening incrementally. On the B2C side – with students buying through retail and online stores – it had little visibility and change was going through an era of ferment, with students choosing to rent rather than buy. In other words, it had a much better sense of what was happening on the supply side than the demand side and that proved a major vulnerability.

In such settings, it is generally a good idea to go to the ultimate user (in this case, a student taking a course) to make sense of the likely future state. Here is the perspective of Coram Williams, Pearson's CFO at the time:

> *The most difficult aspect of these transitions is that if you knew what was really happening, you could respond properly, and yet as a senior management team, you're not sure you understand what's actually going on. Quite often, companies don't do enough in terms of asking the end consumer what's really going on. They rely on their channel partners and resellers, and triangulate from existing data points. My strong advice is get quickly to the end decision maker and understand what they think about what's happening.*

ADVICE TO LEADERS: HOW TO RESPOND TO NEW TECHNOLOGIES

We have talked about the dynamics of technology change and some of the ways companies get it wrong. Now let's broaden the scope to look at the range of strategic options established firms have when faced with disruptive threats.

We have already noted that incumbents are more resilient than most people realize. Recall also the question we asked in the Introduction about the Fortune 500 (*see also* page xx). The data showed that only 24 of the companies in the 2024 Fortune 500 were founded in or after 1995. The other 476 companies had already been around longer and had found ways to adapt to whatever disruptive forces might have come their way. Which begs the question: how did they adapt?

Here is a simple framework to think through the generic options to play with. It is taken from Julian's *Harvard Business Review* article referenced in the previous chapter (*see also* page xx). The top two options are what we call *playing offence*, in other words being proactive and robust in responding to whatever challenge is coming your way. The bottom two are *playing defence*, which means being a bit more indirect and cautious in your response. On the left side we have tactics, which involve focusing on existing markets or segments that you are already strong in, and on the right side we have markets or segments that perhaps you haven't been in before. This suggests four generic options:

FOUR OPTIONS WHEN RESPONDING TO A NEW TECHNOLOGY
OR COMPETITOR

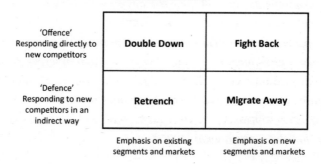

	Emphasis on existing segments and markets	Emphasis on new segments and markets
'Offence' Responding directly to new competitors	Double Down	Fight Back
'Defence' Responding to new competitors in an indirect way	Retrench	Migrate Away

Fight Back

The classic response – almost the knee-jerk reaction – to a new entrant encroaching on your market space is to fight back directly. Plenty of commentators have offered this advice. For example, in the words of Gary Hamel, a colleague at London Business School: '*Out there in some garage is an entrepreneur who's forging a bullet with your company's name on it. You've got one option now – to shoot first. You've got to out-innovate the innovators.*'[6]

We have already talked about the fight-back strategy in some detail – recall the discussion of *Autotrader* in the previous chapter (*see also* page 10) and its stand-alone unit set up to keep the likes of Craigslist and eBay out. Another example is *The New York Times*. From the late 1990s onwards, an array of free online news services sprang up, the likes of *Yahoo!* and, later on, *Huffington Post* and *BuzzFeed*. *The New York Times* quickly put up its own online news-site, initially free and then eventually, after a couple of false starts, with an effective paywall. Today, it has more than 9 million digital subscribers, as well as more than 600,000 print customers – vastly more than it had in the pre-internet era.

Fighting back doesn't necessarily mean creating your own operation to take on the new entrant. Another option is to spend your way out of trouble. Facebook famously bought out its nascent competitors Instagram in 2012 and WhatsApp in 2014, for $1 billion and $19 billion respectively and there are countless examples of these types of strategic acquisitions in the digital world, as well as in renewable energy, pharmaceuticals and other sectors. Other forms of partnerships and joint ventures (e.g. Microsoft investing in OpenAI in 2023), are also available as ways of taking on the new entrant at their own game or simply running them out of town.

What are the risks of fighting back in this way? Depending on how sizeable the technological change is, there is a risk that you don't have the expertise, the speed or the commitment to react quickly enough. Nokia and BlackBerry were unable to bring a touch-screen phone to market quickly following the 2007 launch of the iPhone – they simply didn't have the technological expertise. Or consider a very different industry, airlines. Way back in the 1990s, British Airways created a separate unit called Go to fight back against Ryanair and EasyJet. It attracted a reasonable number of customers but because of its ties to BA, it couldn't get its costs low enough to compete and never became profitable. BA eventually sold it to EasyJet in 2002.

Double Down

Every incumbent company has an array of valuable assets and capabilities – brands, distribution facilities, relationships. When faced with a potentially disruptive threat, the best way forward is sometimes to double down on those assets and use them even more effectively than before.

Consider how Disney responded to the emergence of digital video streaming, first with YouTube in 2005 and then with Netflix and Amazon Video in 2008. Disney was keenly aware that this was happening and that a new form of movie distribution was potentially threatening to its existing business model. So, did Disney 'fight back' with a digital streaming service of its own? No, it didn't. Instead, it doubled down on movie production, buying out Pixar and acquiring Marvel and Lucasfilm to give it a market-leading position in the creation of high-quality content. This gave it a very strong bargaining position with the streaming services such as Netflix. As the streaming market grew and matured, Disney decided to enter with Disney+ in 2019. At the time of writing, Disney had some 200 million subscribers, though it is debatable how profitable streaming is – for Disney and indeed for the industry as a whole.

Another example, closer to home for us, is how leading business schools responded to the threat of online learning. London Business School, like its competitors, always saw itself as a provider of high-quality, in-person learning. In the early 2010s online programme managers (OPMs) started to grow aggressively, offering high-quality online courses for business executives, often using well-known faculty and at much lower prices than the in-person offerings of top business schools. At London Business School, they debated whether to compete directly with these OPMs and concluded that they should not. Instead, they offered online courses selectively and built their expertise in developing them so that they could offer 'blended' learning that combined in-person and online. But they believed then – as they do now – that in-person learning provides a higher-quality experience than anything you can do remotely. So far, this assessment has proved correct.

What are the risks of the double-down strategy? The big risk of course is that your assets and capabilities are no longer valued in the marketplace. Kodak had undeniable expertise in manufacturing, marketing and selling film, all of which turned out to be worthless in the digital imaging world. But we would argue Kodak faced a very unusual set of circumstances. The more common scenario is where some of your assets become irrelevant, but others remain powerful. Consider what happened to the big pharma players like Pfizer and AstraZeneca, when drug development was taken over by biotechnology. These large players needed to partner with biotechs to gain access to the latest drug technologies. But the biotechs needed big pharma in return, for clinical trials, regulatory approval, global distribution and the like. It turned out that these complementary assets in the downstream part of business system were sufficiently important that Pfizer, AstraZeneca and others had time to build up their biotechnology expertise. This is why the big pharma companies have come through the biotechnology revolution in good shape.

Retrench
Sometimes an emerging technology is sufficiently threatening that you must take a step back. Faced with an invading army, you cede some territory, but you consolidate and protect your remaining strongholds. That's what we mean by a retrench strategy. It is sometimes similar to doubling-down, in that you focus on your existing strengths, but it's done from a position of weakness, not strength.

There are many tactics available, all designed to shore up an existing business as effectively as possible. You can cut costs. You can merge with other competitors. You can lobby governments to change the regulatory regime. All these tactics are designed to increase your economies of scale and scope, and to make sure whoever the insurgent competitor is, they cannot scale your walls.

One example of retrenching is the UK newsagent, WH Smith. Back in the early days of the online revolution, WH Smith faced an important decision: should it go online? Every other retailer was creating an online presence at that time, though with mixed levels of success. But WH Smith, under the leadership of Kate Swann, decided not to. Instead, Swann decided to focus the company back on its core business, which was its retail shops in high-traffic areas like airports, train stations and major high streets. She sold their newspaper distribution business and closed some peripheral outlets. Essentially, the strategy was to squeeze as much value out of their retail footprint as possible. Which meant adding higher-margin bottles of water and candy bars at the till, automating the checkouts and keeping costs low.

How did this strategy work out? From 2002 until the mid-2010s revenues decreased and profits increased *every single year*. That's an impressive trick to pull off, increasing your profits in absolute terms while your revenues are being squeezed. But obviously there are limits to how long you can keep this going. Subsequently, from the late 2010s on, WH Smith started growing its revenues again, expanding into a number of international locations (mostly at airports), and investing heavily in technology to automate and simplify a lot of their back-office processes.

What are the risks of this strategy? The biggest one is that you are telling a story people do not want to hear. If you were to say to your shareholders: we see this internet thing coming and actually, we don't think it's for us, we aren't going to bother with it, we will just do what we've always done, that would not go down well! Yet in some ways, that's exactly what WH Smith did. And we are confident that, in this specific case, they made more money for their shareholders than if they had tried to build an online business or diversify in some other way.

Migrate Away
Unlike the first three strategies, which are all about making money from where you are or where the new competitor is coming from, this involves seeking your future elsewhere. It's essentially a portfolio play – if you look across all your business areas and you see one where the competition is heating up because of a technology disruption, it sometimes makes sense to cash in and invest in a more secure or attractive market somewhere else.

Fujifilm, Kodak's big competitor back in the late 1990s when digital imaging was first taking off, is a good example of this approach. We know Kodak failed and Fujifilm survived, so why was that? Fujifilm were smart enough – or perhaps lucky enough – to have kept the chemical business that was the basis of their original line of film products so as film sales started to decline, Fujifilm began to diversify – first into cosmetics and then subsequently into pharmaceuticals. It is still a successful company to this day, though its product line is dramatically different to what it was 20 years ago.

Another example is the Canadian company, Thomson Corporation. Back in the late 1990s, Thomson was a diversified company with oil and gas assets and a range of newspaper holdings, including the *Daily Telegraph* in the UK and the *Globe and Mail* in Canada. In 1999, Chairman Ken Thomson sold off the newspaper portfolio and refocused the company on digital information services, ultimately buying out UK information service provider Reuters in 2007. Rather than battle it out in the newspaper industry, he migrated the company away to a new place. And with impressive results – throughout the 2010s Thomson Reuters was one of the highest-performing companies on the Canadian stock market.

Is migrating away a sure-fire way of succeeding? Of course not, because any diversification move is risky – out of the frying pan into the fire, as they say. But the traditional photo film and newspaper industries were in sufficiently dire places that Fujifilm and Thomson made the right decisions at the time.

Making choices

Which of these options should you pursue? It depends on your circumstances. For example, if you have strong assets that the market still values, doubling down on your existing strategy is likely to work out well. If digitization is a threat that you're not well-positioned to counter, moving away into new defensible areas is probably the smart bet. There are benefits and risks to each of these strategies (see table below).

TABLE 2.1: SUMMARY OF BENEFITS AND RISKS FOR EACH STRATEGY

	Economic logic	*Examples*	*Risks*
Fight Back	Creative destruction, disruptive innovation	*New York Times, Autotrader*	Moving too late/too slow, misreading an emerging trend; hard to execute well
Double Down	Resource view, time compression diseconomies	Disney, Pfizer	Market may not value your existing assets in the future
Retrench	Economies of scale and scope, barriers to entry, protectionism	WH Smith, Penguin Books	Likely leads to long-term decline; hard to sell to stakeholders
Migrate Away	Core competencies, Real options	Thomson, Fujifilm	Out of the frying pan into the fire; diversification is always hard

Can you do all four at the same time? That makes sense up to a point – when a new technology or upstart competitor first comes along, you need to understand the context, do some careful analysis and consider a full range of options.

Consider Pearson's response to Amazon's Kindle, which was launched with a big fanfare in 2007. Pearson owned Penguin, one of six major book publishers. Coram Williams, Pearson's CFO at the time, told us:

> *Book publishing had not changed for decades. Overnight, the Kindle threatened that, because it changed the delivery, marketing and sale of content. One of our concerns was that it offered a real chance, for the first time, to disintermediate publishers. Our biggest fear was that Amazon would see themselves as the publisher.*

What was Pearson's response to the Kindle? One strategy was a shift into self-publishing, to mitigate the threat that Amazon would seek to disintermediate their relationship with authors. In 2012, as noted in the previous chapter (*see also* page 15), Pearson acquired Author Solutions, a leader in the niche self-publishing industry. However, this business never took off. It became clear that authors continued to value the service provided by traditional publishing houses like Penguin and it turned out that Amazon did not have ambitions to become a book publisher. Pearson sold Author Solutions in 2016 to a private equity company, Najafi.

The other strategy was a merger of Penguin with Random House, one of the other big-six publishers, which went through in 2013. Coram Williams explained the thinking behind this:

> *Amazon's Kindle changed the power balance in the book publishing industry. E-book sales suddenly took off. The risk was if the trajectory continued, we would end up in a market where the largest publisher had about 15 per cent market share and Amazon (as an e-book distributor) had 90 per cent share.*

Faced with this threat, Pearson saw that shifting market power in the other direction would be beneficial, so a deal with Random House was engineered. This gave the merged entity approximately 30 per cent market share in publishing and at times more than that in the bestseller charts. As Coram said, 'The risk of Amazon saying, *as we cannot agree on terms, we are going to turn off over 30 per cent of our content,* was low.'

In the terminology of this chapter, Penguin therefore pursued a dual strategy – fighting back through self-publishing and retrenching through a merger. And we can see similar tactics playing out in other industries.

For example, consider J.P. Morgan's response to cryptocurrency – simultaneously 'waging a war of words' against the new technology while joining a consortium of banks to investigate it, and then subsequently investing in it directly.[7] Or look at Fiat Chrysler's stance towards autonomous vehicles – partnering with upstarts Aptiv and Waymo, a consortium with BMW, Intel and Mobileye, while also pursuing a full-blown merger with France's PSA. In conditions of high ambiguity, hedging your bets makes sense.

However – and this is an important point – you eventually need to come off the fence. Strategy is, by definition, a commitment to a course of action that precludes others and a failure to choose can be fatal. Consider Kodak again. When digital photography became possible, it could have retrenched around its declining but profitable photo/film business (and paid shareholders dividends for another decade); or gone all-in on digital imaging or sought pastures new, as Fujifilm did. Instead, a succession of CEOs tried a bit of everything, resulting in confused customers and a premature end.

Companies active in a range of industries may make different decisions in different parts of their portfolios. For example, as the challenges of digital disruption grew, Pearson decided that it needed to 'fight back' in each of its three major areas of business – education, trade publishing and news & information – but that it didn't have the scale, bandwidth or financial capacity to pursue that strategy simultaneously in three different industries, with varying market dynamics in each one. Therefore, over time, Pearson exited two of the three areas. It sold the *Financial Times* to Nikkei and its stakes in Penguin Random House and The Economist Group to its respective joint venture partners, raising £3.2 billion in total from selling businesses that made £156 million in annual operating profits. It then used that £3.2 billion to finance its digital transformation in education, shifting from being an analogue content publisher to a digital learning and certification company, and strengthening its balance sheet by paying down debt. As we'll discuss in a later chapter, a strong balance sheet is particularly important for a public company during a major digital disruption. It gives shareholders confidence that the company has the financial strength to invest in fast-growing, but not yet highly profitable digital businesses while managing declining but still profitable analogue ones – without them having to worry that it might go bankrupt in the interim.

DYNAMICS OF CREATIVE DESTRUCTION

Our focus here has been on the incumbent company and how it responds to a digital threat but there is another variable to throw into the mix as well, namely the motivation and capability of the new players who are seeking to disrupt the status quo. Sometimes the new entrants are small entrepreneurial outfits looking for a foothold, sometimes they are experienced, professional teams with deep-pocketed backers and sometimes it's one of the big-tech players such as Amazon or Google.

The strategies of the big-tech players are well-known and we discussed one specific example (Amazon's foray into trade publishing) already. But let's look a little closer at the venture capital-backed startups that emerged in many sectors over the last 15 years.

An important feature of such companies has been a huge appetite for risk on the part of their investors. As long as these startups were able to achieve top-line sales growth, the investment continued to pour in. This created a difficult short-term dynamic as they typically spent a fortune on customer acquisition, damaging profitability for all. Incumbent competitors could see this was going on, but they didn't know how long the venture-backed startups would keep it up. This meant they had a difficult story to tell their own board or investors in the meantime.

The key point we would make to incumbents is – hold your nerve. We started working on the ideas in this book in 2021, at a time when venture capital-backed startups were generating spectacular valuations. But the laws of gravity eventually asserted themselves, so that by the time we completed the book in 2024, the world looked very different. Of course, some fast-growing startups become hugely successful, but in most cases something went awry. A few examples:

> *Dollar Shave Club.* This was one of the most visible direct to consumer (DTC) consumer goods companies, who succeeded in building a strong following for their monthly subscription service, thanks in part to an irreverent and humorous marketing campaign, with the result that Unilever bought them for $1 billion in 2016. But their success was fleeting. While there was – and continues to be – a market for subscription-based shaving services, it's actually quite a small niche. The majority of men, it turns out, are happy to buy their Gillette razors from the local supermarket. Unilever sold Dollar Shave Club to a private equity buyer in 2021 for an undisclosed sum.[8]

2U. This Boston-based online education business grew rapidly through the 2010s, with a peak market value of $5 billion in 2018. Seeking to become the big player in the sector, it bought out competitors like edX, Trilogy Education and GetSmarter. But there was a fundamental mismatch between its vision – to be the platform powering online learning, directing millions of learners to the right course for them – and the much narrower role it actually played – doing the outsourced enrolment marketing for universities in a series of stand-alone, time-limited contracts. While demand for online learning continues to grow, 2U underestimated the desire of bricks-and-mortar universities to retain control of their own digital strategies. There was a temporary reprieve during the pandemic, but faced with the realities of a business model that was never profitable, it lost shareholder support. In June 2024, 2U filed for chapter 11 bankruptcy.

Babylon Health Services. Founded by Ali Parsa in 2013, it sought to revolutionize healthcare through virtual consultations and clever AI. It grew rapidly, through contracts with the NHS in England and various medical insurers in the US. But the complexity of the healthcare system, and the overhyped technology, made Babylon's business model far less effective than envisioned. It had a peak market capitalization of $4 billion and at the time of writing, it was worthless.[9]

WeWork. This story is so well known that we won't repeat it here.[10] Its charismatic CEO, Adam Neumann, somehow persuaded a group of sophisticated investors, most notably Masa Son at Softbank, that buying up long leases on Manhattan properties and selling that space on short-term leases to corporate clients was a viable business model. From its peak valuation of $47 billion, WeWork filed for Chapter 11 bankruptcy in 2023.

We're not suggesting you generalize from these four examples because there are some well-funded startups that successfully make inroads into their chosen market but it's worth keeping these cautionary tales in mind. Echoing what we said in Chapter 1, you must accept the possibility that these aggressive new entrants might 'eat your lunch' but knowing that the odds are still generally on your side over the medium to long term.

It's also worth underlining that the last 15 years have been very unusual, in the sense that interest rates were close to zero, so venture capital and private equity companies were particularly keen to take on risky ventures that might offer them some sort of return on their money. In today's business world, where interest rates are around 5 per cent at the time of writing, there is less 'dumb money' around and there are fewer aggressively-backed startups to worry about. For example, the next wave of AI-inspired digital disruption is being led by Big Tech itself and a smaller, tighter group of startups, many of whom are aligned with the big technology companies. This brings its own set of challenges for industrial incumbents, which we'll discuss in Chapter 7.

GETTING THE TIMING RIGHT – SOME FINAL THOUGHTS

Looking across all these examples of how companies respond to new technologies, we can draw out some important themes. The key point is that the pace of digital change is uneven and uncertain. There are some things you can control but a lot you can't, and you must learn to deal with it.

The example at the beginning of this chapter – the new iPad delivered curriculum for American schools – was a case of Pearson getting too far ahead of our customers, leaving analogue dollars on the table for smaller, less digitally focused competitors to pick up. There have also been times when Pearson hung on too long to product and business models that it felt comfortable with but were past their sell-by date.

But, even when you do get your timing right, the short-term financial impact can be hard to forecast. For example, in the next chapter, we will talk in detail about transitioning away from traditional college textbooks to a digital first model. Pearson's earnings guidance to the capital markets, which anticipated the move, assumed that students would continue to shift at a somewhat accelerated rate to the new model. What John and his team didn't anticipate was that the announcement would shift students buying behaviour to the lower-priced digital product at a much faster rate, especially those previously still buying the most expensive bundled print and digital product. This was good news for the business longer term – the quicker Pearson got to a fully digital, access style world, the quicker the pain of the secondary market would be behind it. But the immediate, in-year impact led to a profits warning for the company, damaging management credibility with the capital markets.

In summary, here are three key take-aways when confronting an uncertain future:

- You need a clear vision of what the digital-first future for your company looks like and drive consistently towards that.
- You need to accept that the customer will play a big part in determining the pacing of that digital shift and often it goes more slowly than you expect for some years before then going more quickly.
- And if you're a public company with annual earnings expectations, managing shareholder communications through this transition can be hugely challenging.

This dynamic – that it is often easier to see what the end state of the digital transition looks like than foresee the quarter by quarter or year by year ups and downs in getting there – is what makes the pacing of the analogue to digital shift so difficult to manage, especially for publicly listed companies. But it mustn't inhibit you as leaders from having a clear vision and driving relentlessly towards it.

Timing is a huge part of the story when it comes to digital transformation but it is also important to get the fundamentals right, in terms of defining a business model that is fit for purpose in an increasingly digital business environment. That's the challenge we will turn to in the next chapter.

3

Digital Business Models: New Ways to Make Money

The digital revolution has shaken many industries and often through fundamental structural changes. In the previous chapter, we focused on process and timing issues to help you think more rigorously about when you respond to emerging technologies. In this chapter, our focus shifts towards the nature of the change and specifically on the types of business models that succeed in a digitally enabled ecosystem. Here, we provide a map of the evolving landscape across different industries and the emerging models that are proving successful. In the second half of the chapter, we offer a framework to help you think about opportunities to reinvent your own business model.

FINDING YOUR PLACE IN THE DIGITAL WORLD – LESSONS FROM PEARSON

At Pearson, it seemed that in every internal meeting John took part colleagues would be talking about what the company's platform strategy should be. This anxiety was created by the huge growth and exceptional power wielded by the 'Magnificent Seven' tech companies. Everyone wanted to see if they could get a piece of the 'platform action'. They were worried that their business model would be broken by Amazon, Google or some unknown venture capital-backed startup.

One of the lessons Pearson discovered was that when people talk about platform strategy, they often use the same words to describe three very different things: 'Replatforming' the company, being a platform company and engaging with a platform owned by somebody else. It causes huge confusion when the term 'platform strategy' is used interchangeably to describe all three.

Let's separate out these three different concepts. **Replatforming** typically refers to changes an incumbent company makes to its IT infrastructure – for example, decommissioning legacy technology and moving to the Cloud to improve, among other things, the user experience. You need to do this, to be able to comprehend and make sense of the huge amounts of customer data and insight in your own system, so you can be truly digital and mobile first in a sustainable, scalable way. It can be a hugely costly and disruptive undertaking and we will discuss it in more detail in Chapter 5 when we focus on digital infrastructure.

Other incumbents have a real aspiration to **be a platform in their own right** with large numbers of users attracted to them, perhaps initially for one purpose, and are then persuaded to stay with them for a wider engagement. It is this ambition and the allure of capital market valuations reflective of the wider platform approach that has led so many companies to aspire to be the 'next' Netflix or the 'next' Spotify of a whole plethora of different industries but this is a very hard thing for incumbents to pull off.

In the media sector – for example, Disney – because of its brand, the breadth of its highly valued content and its financial strength – is one of the few incumbents with a real opportunity to build a successful streaming platform of its own. Disney's competitors, such as Universal and Paramount, have found it much harder to compete with Netflix and Amazon Prime Video. Indeed, it seems to be harder for content companies to become a platform than it is for platform companies to start creating content. Consider each of the three major Pearson businesses at the time when John became CEO: the *Financial Times*, Penguin and Pearson Education. Each had its own brand, but none had the breadth of offering, or strength required to build a platform in the style of Netflix or Spotify.

- As much as *Financial Times* readers value its premium content, it will rarely be their sole or even primary source of news and information. They will also consume content from CNN, *The New York Times*, the *Wall Street Journal*, the BBC, the *Washington Post*, the *Economist* and the like.
- In trade publishing, discovery is very important. This refers to how readers decide what books to buy by browsing in a bookstore or through online search behaviour; the reviews they read, the recommendations they get. Readers buy books by title, author, celebrity, book cover, review, word of mouth, or movie tie-in. They very rarely buy imprints and no one publisher or imprint can offer the required range of discovery.
- As for textbooks, an American college student may have two or three courses that are dependent on Pearson content, but they'll have at least as many again that are dependent on some combination of Pearson's competitors: McGraw-Hill, Wiley, Cengage, Oxford University Press or Macmillan.

In short, consumers are less likely to sign up to a platform that cannot meet most of their needs. And in each of these cases, the Pearson businesses fell short. Equally, these businesses were highly unlikely to join a platform that was owned by a major rival, because they did not trust each other to play fair.

As Pearson discovered in college publishing, attempts by rivals to launch a new commonly owned platform could be short-lived. CourseSmart was founded in 2007 by Pearson along with Macmillan, Cengage, Wiley and McGraw-Hill. It offered access to e-text via web browser, allowing readers to read e-books rather than physical textbooks. Readers had access to both downloadable and online versions. They subsequently launched apps for iPhone, iPad and Android devices. By 2014, the company had partnered with around 50 publishers and provided well over half of the e-textbooks used in higher education.

Despite being one of the two largest eBook providers at the time, CourseSmart was losing money and required further investment. Some of its owners were under severe financial pressure with one filing for Chapter 11 protection from bankruptcy. These publishers did not want to continue to invest in a small loss-making startup and were reluctant to continue to supply products to the platform if it was then fully owned by one of their direct competitors.

In any event, as the business grew, anti-trust issues relating to how the competing publishers engaged with each other through the platform became more challenging. The business was sold to VitalSource, which is now the world's leading platform for digital textbooks. It's an example of how hard it is for product companies to remake themselves as a platform, even if they do try to work collaboratively with their competitors.

The third type of platform strategy, then, is **engaging with a platform owned by somebody else**, and we will have a lot more to say on it in the pages ahead. While engaging with someone else's platform sounds less attractive than orchestrating your own, there are many ways of making it work. As Annette Thomas, former CEO of the Guardian Media Group, put it to us:

> *Being really clear whether you're in a position to create a platform strategy versus participate in a broader ecosystem is probably one of the most important strategic questions to get right early on. Participating as well in somebody else's platform is not necessarily a bad place to be, if you've got a brand that people want to access anyway. It's not a bad place to be, but you do have to be very conscious of how that ecosystem is developing over time.*

EXAMPLES FROM OTHER SECTORS

Looking beyond the world of media and publishing, let's consider how the shift towards digital platforms has affected other industries. Many incumbent companies have struggled to find the right formula. Here are three well-known examples.

Toys 'R' Us. Everybody remembers Toys 'R' Us as the big out-of-town toy store that grew rapidly through the 1980s and 1990s. In 2000, Toys 'R' Us executives decided to do a deal with Amazon, essentially to use it as their online shopping channel alongside their physical stores. This was the period when the internet was starting to explode, with Amazon, among others, starting to dominate certain sectors of the online market. But no one could have foreseen back then just how dominant Amazon might become.

Toys 'R' Us saw their core competency as bricks-and-mortar retailing. This new channel called the internet seemed important, but perhaps not critical to their survival: who didn't want to take their kids to buy toys in a big store? So Toys 'R' Us signed an exclusive 10-year deal, whereby Amazon would be their sole online distributor and Toys 'R' Us would be the sole provider of toys on Amazon's platform. However, it quickly became apparent that Amazon had vastly more ambition than Toys 'R' Us had anticipated. Amazon started working with other companies selling toys and adjacent products and they began making and selling their own competing products online. These moves went explicitly against the exclusive deal that they had signed with Toys 'R' Us. Although Toys 'R' Us won their court case in 2006, it was too late for them to regain the ground they had lost.

Toys 'R' Us was already in trouble by 2005 and ultimately filed for bankruptcy in 2017. While there were many factors behind their demise, the heart of the problem was they never built an online strategy of their own and they yielded too much space to Amazon.

General Electric. A very different example is GE (General Electric), for many years the most valuable company in the world. It was an industrial and financial conglomerate, producing everything from aircraft engines to medical equipment, to power systems, to trains.

Around the early 2000s when the internet was taking off, Jeff Immelt, the chief executive at the time, decided that GE needed to become a digital company. He saw the digitization trends and he realized it would not just affect consumer products, but industrial products too.

His 'nightmare scenario' was essentially what had happened to Toys 'R' Us, namely that GE might allow another provider to build a technology platform, with GE ending up playing second fiddle.

So, Immelt made a big bet. He created GE Digital, the centrepiece of which was a technology platform called Predix. At an abstract level, Predix was envisioned as the equivalent of iOS (the Apple operating system) or Windows for industrial products. The idea was that GE would create and control this platform on which information about – for example, engineering equipment would be placed so that they would avoid somebody else coming in and disintermediating them from their customers.

Now, in some ways this was brilliant and farsighted, but ultimately it was the wrong move because they pushed too hard to create a platform the world was not ready for. It became all things to all people; it was not specific enough to their engineering business, their transportation business, or their medical equipment business. As a result, GE ended up with something which never really took off. Other companies were not prepared to work with them and GE never recouped their costs. Of course, GE was eventually broken up in 2024 into three separate and more focused companies. The failure of GE Digital wasn't the only reason for GE being demerged, but it was a significant contributor.

iTunes. A third cautionary tale, as touched on earlier, is the new business model that never was. In the late 1990s there were four major music publishers: Sony, Warner, EMI and Universal. In theory, they might have created a platform themselves on which they could have sold their music. In practice, they were unable to come together. Sony, for example, worked very hard to create an online music store, first through PressPlay and then through the Connect Music platform. But the obstacles were huge. There was initially no impetus for them to collaborate as a joint platform would have hurt their profitability. And of course, the four parties each had their own ideas about how a joint platform might work.

This left the door open to new entrants. The file sharing service, Napster, had given people the ability to download music, illegally, for free. While the record labels did everything they could to protect their existing business model by taking legal action against Napster and 'locking' CDs and online music files virtually using digital rights management tools, it wasn't enough to hold back the tides of change and Apple CEO Steve Jobs saw an opportunity.

The lesson Jobs drew from Napster was not that people wanted to access music for free, but rather that they wanted to download songs they liked in an affordable and easy way rather than drive to a record store to buy CDs. As the record industry couldn't offer an affordable, easy and legal way of doing this, Apple did. Jobs persuaded the record labels – starting with Warner Music – to make iTunes their digital storefront.

A few years later, iTunes was itself disrupted by Spotify, which enabled consumers to access millions of songs by paying a monthly fee to stream them from the Cloud-based service. The 'content agnostic' position taken by Apple, then later Spotify, as outsiders gave them a huge advantage in the eyes of consumers, leaving the major music publishers to rue a missed opportunity.

Media investment analyst, Patrick Wellington, who has covered the music industry since the 1990s, gave us his colourful take on this episode:

Steve Jobs came along and invented Apple iTunes and the music industry should have got down on bended knee and thanked him for saving their business because suddenly you didn't have to pirate. It was a legitimate and pleasant experience to consume music digitally.

But the music industry hated Steve Jobs. They thought he was stealing their business in the same way as the music video people had. Then the subscription model came along. With all due respect to current music businesses, you can argue that what's made them successful is that whole interrelationship with the consumer has been taken entirely out of their hands. Now they rely on Spotify and Apple Music and all the other platforms to deliver the customers and to deliver their growth and they can go back to what the music companies arguably do best, which is selecting, managing, editing, curating and allowing that whole interface with the customer to happen elsewhere.

STRATEGIC OPTIONS FOR OPERATING ON SOMEONE ELSE'S PLATFORM

The reality for most incumbents is that new platform companies are going to emerge in your space and you are much more likely to find yourself part of *their* ecosystem than to be the centre of the ecosystem yourself. Which begs a key question: how do you operate as part of a wider ecosystem, engaging with one or more powerful platforms? In our experience, there are three ways to go:

Bypass the Platform

First, you can try to bypass the platform entirely. In some cases, your digital product and brand may be strong enough that you can skirt round the platform completely or partially until you have gained real digital scale.

For example, back in 2011, the *Financial Times* developed its own web app and pulled its dedicated iOS apps from Apple's App Store. Why? It did not want to pay 30 per cent of its revenues to Apple and it wanted to know more about its subscribers than Apple was willing to share. Additionally, because of the strength of the *FT* brand, and the fact that it was largely migrating existing loyal readers from print to digital, it was not overly reliant on the App Store for customers to discover its product.

Six years later, with its own digital presence established, the *FT* was able to migrate back to the iOS App and was thus able to negotiate better commercial terms with Apple. An important reason to migrate back to Apple was that the 'native' app (the one specifically designed for iOS) delivered a superior user experience; one that enables the *FT* to extend its reach well beyond its existing readership. The *FT* was also now able to collect significant data on its core user base, something it would have been unable to do, had it not established its own independent digital presence.

Build Bargaining Power

This gets us to the second strategy for countering a strong platform provider, namely building up your own bargaining power.

We discussed the merger of Penguin and Random House in the previous chapter as a way of countering Amazon's dominant position in e-book distribution. By way of context, in 2014, there was a huge conflict between Amazon and the trade publisher Hachette over who controlled the retail price of their books. For a time, Amazon opted to 'go dark' on Hachette, meaning that it refused to list Hachette's books on its website, until eventually a compromise was reached. As Coram Williams told us:

> We had some very difficult negotiations as a combined company with Amazon but although they threatened to 'go dark' and turn off our content they never did and I think that was because they understood that you cannot deliver a platform to your customers and then cut off 30 per cent – or sometimes more – of what they want. It just doesn't work.
>
> There are many reasons why I think trade publishing has been one of the few media businesses that has seen a successful digital transformation, but one of the key ones was the re-establishment of market power and equilibrium between Amazon, and the publishers. And Penguin Random House was a big part of that.

Another example is how Pearson managed its learning offering for students. Consider a student who is assigned a course through Pearson's online homework platform. There is no place for discovery as the professor tells them what they need. There is no substitute and the way to buy the product at the lowest price is directly from Pearson. This in turn creates an opportunity to sell them other products. Thus, Pearson was able to build up a reasonable level of customer loyalty, making its negotiation with Apple and Android over commercial terms more palatable.

From this direct engagement with millions of learners, Pearson was then able to launch an online offering, Pearson+. This was highly unlikely to ever be a fully-fledged platform as a 'Spotify of education'. However, it helped to counterbalance the power of VitalSource and other emerging platforms that were trying to aggregate the digital learning products of all publishers.

This example highlights a related point; that the emergence of new digital and e-commerce platforms can be hugely beneficial for incumbents. In trade publishing, for example, it has significantly enhanced the value of the backlist (what in music is called the back catalogue) – the long tail of products that sell in small volumes – as these are now much easier to discover online.

Differentiate and innovate

The third option for incumbents is to innovate and differentiate and create value for end consumers. This ensures customers will continue to engage with you directly as well as through third-party platforms. Again, there are several examples from Pearson:

- Pearson built its own data and insight team both to analyse and interpret data and to engage more effectively, both with its own consumers and with Amazon, seeking win-win opportunities to work together.
- The *Financial Times* used ft.com to engage more deeply with its audiences, build online communities around industry verticals through podcasts, videos, in-person online events and conferences built around specific themes, always with the goal of deepening relationships with readers directly.
- Penguin Random House created author websites and podcasts, online book groups and special interest groups that diffused dependency and gave the company the direct access to the user insight and engagement that Amazon was often reluctant to share.
- Pearson+ used its platform to establish a direct relationship with the 10 million plus learners per year who relied on its online homework and related platforms. The learners were directed to Pearson+ by their college professors. They would continue to engage with the platform only if Pearson gave them a compelling reason to do so; through access to online tutoring

and study prep, links to industry experts, a recommendation
engine directing them along the pathway to the career of their
dreams. Pearson is now using this platform to launch its own
AI powered personalized learning applications.

In summary, these are the three options for working around or with a
large platform player like Amazon or Google. You can seek to bypass
the platform completely, you can enhance your own bargaining power
in engaging with the platform, and you can innovate and differentiate
in ways that engage customers directly with you, as well as through
the platforms by which they buy their products.

At some point in a digital transformation journey, most incumbent
companies will pursue a strategy that combines elements of all three.
They will also discover that their capabilities and those of the platform companies can be compatible, to mutual benefit. Consider for
example how Penguin Random House found a way of working with
Amazon. Madeline McIntosh, former CEO of its North American
business, shared her reflections with us:

> When we first started meeting with Amazon, it was with Jeff
> Bezos himself, in our conference room, and we were trying to
> figure out exactly what kind of a company this is, trying to
> understand whether we should be concerned or not.
>
> What became apparent was that Amazon mastered data,
> online merchandising, metadata, optimization, pricing, far
> quicker than we were able to and so rapidly became a dominant
> force in books and a huge threat to us.
>
> What we figured out in parallel, however, was whilst
> transacting on a platform such as Amazon is much more
> efficient and generates much better cash flows, we could still
> take responsibility for generating demand.
>
> It turned out that all those old-fashioned skills of publishing,
> sales and editorial, which are by nature very instinctive, were
> still important. Cases where our publishers and editors are able
> to say 'there's nothing based on history, there's nothing in the
> data and nothing in past sales reports that will show this new

*book is going to be successful, and that it even has the potential
to change lives, but I am telling you this book will be a hit'.*

*Those were the magical moments that we saw and that only
came from people with decades of experience. Incorporating
this internal feedback and working with interest groups and
consumer insights panels really allowed us to get a much better
feel for the market.*

*This was how we figured out which way to pivot and
incorporate Amazon into our business, whilst really investing in
our publishing and editorial teams, sales and marketing teams,
and building out our own supply chain to turn Penguin Random
House into one of the biggest trade publishers in the world.*

DIGITALLY DRIVEN BUSINESS MODEL INNOVATION – A CONCEPTUAL FRAMEWORK

These examples from Pearson and other companies are hopefully
useful for you as you think about your own strategy for working with
these big digital platforms that dominate today's business landscape.
But we want to go a bit further in this chapter, by giving you a framework and some practical advice to help you with your own attempts
at digital transformation. What follows next is an exercise we have
done many times with students and executives to help them think in
fresh ways about business model innovation. The box below provides
a quick reminder of the terms we use in this exercise, to make sure
everyone is on the same page.

BUSINESS MODEL INNOVATION – DEFINITION OF TERMS

A *business model* is a 'formula for making money' – it is the choices
you make about how you generate revenue, what you spend money
on, what you do yourself versus what you use partners to do for you.
Within a given industry there may be several business models (e.g. the
full-service airline like British Airways alongside the no-frills, low-cost
service offered by airlines such as Ryanair or Southwest Airlines).

A *business model innovation* is a new way of making money in an existing industry. Ikea famously reinvented the furniture industry by taking out one whole step in the value-chain (the furniture manufacturer). Southwest Airlines and Ryanair pioneered the no-frills airline model. These innovations did not rely on digital technology, but increasingly the most important opportunities for business model innovation arise from technological changes.

A *platform* is simply a medium through which parties interact. Uber brings together drivers and passengers (riders). Facebook brings together people with personal stories to tell and advertisers who want to reach them. Most platforms are technology enabled, making use of the reach of the internet to bring parties together, but the concept applies equally to 'analogue' equivalents such as flea markets and nightclubs.

An *ecosystem* is a constellation of organizations who work together in some collaborative fashion to create value for a particular group of users. Ecosystems typically have a central player – the spider in the web – such as Google, Apple or Amazon that orchestrates the efforts of others. And again, while the notion of an ecosystem has taken off in the digital era, there are industrial-era ecosystems as well, such as tiers of suppliers that feed into Toyota or Volkswagen's production systems.

A popular way of talking about business model innovation is the notion of a *Blue Ocean Strategy*,[1] whereby a company creates new user value – for example, through a better experience, higher quality, better service or dramatically lower cost. A successful Blue Ocean Strategy gives a company access to new demand, a previously uncolonized market space and an opportunity to make vast profits at least for a period of time in marked contrast to the Red Ocean Strategy where companies fight among themselves to grab a share of existing demand.

So where do blue ocean strategies come from? Looking at many well-known cases over the years, there are broadly two ways they emerge.

One is a **creative breakthrough** by an entrepreneur – for example, Ingvar Kamprad coming up with the revolution in furniture design/ assembly that made Ikea the world leading company it is today, or Cirque du Soleil, the Montreal-based company that reinvented the circus for the modern era.

The other, and our primary focus here, is a **technology-enabled breakthrough**. The internet is, of course, the most important of these and there are plenty of other digital technologies that are also part of the story but it's worth noting that there are non-digital technologies that can also enable business model innovation. The automobile industry is an obvious example. The reason battery-powered electric vehicles took off is because the lithium-ion battery, which had existed before, became a very powerful way of storing enough power to run a car for 300 miles without a recharge. Elon Musk himself, the Tesla founder, was one of the pioneers in taking this technology and figuring out a way of incorporating it into a car. Through his innovations, he has transformed the car industry through a new vertically integrated business model.

It should be clear that the creative breakthrough by an entrepreneur and a technology-enabled breakthrough often go hand-in-hand – examples would be Jeff Bezos selling books online, Steve Jobs inventing the iPhone and Allen Zhang launching WeChat. But it's still very useful to separate them out at a conceptual level.

So how do *you* come up with a technology-enabled breakthrough? Of course it's not easy – if it were easy, someone else would have done it already. But one helpful way forward is through a structured conversation looking at approaches that have been used by others and seeing how they can be applied in your case. Here is our way of characterizing the different ways digital technology enables business model innovation for incumbents.

The User Perspective

Taking a user or customer perspective of your business is the oldest idea out there. Peter Drucker, the original management guru, said that the job of business is to 'create a customer'[2], everything else is secondary to that. Indeed, there are entire schools of thought – for example, design thinking – that are about trying to tap into unmet or even unarticulated user needs and to find a way of meeting them.

Henry Ford famously said, 'If I had asked my customers what they wanted, they would have just said they wanted a faster horse.' When Steve Jobs was asked if he had done any market research before launching the iPhone he replied: 'Well, did Alexander Graham Bell do any market research when he first introduced the telephone?' Stated differently, you do not just ask customers what they want, you try to truly understand and tap into their underlying needs to create products or services which they would want even if they don't know that they want them. There are two aspects of taking a user perspective. One is service-based and the other is outcome-based.

#1. Service-Based Models. This is the idea that alongside a product, we are selling value-added services. When you buy a car, you are offered a financing package, a warranty and insurance package, and a variety of optional extras that you probably don't want. The services sold with the car are usually more profitable than the car itself, from the point of view of the manufacturer or dealer, so it's very much in their interests to sell you the complete bundle.

Another example is Domino's Pizza, which has been very proactive in the use of digital technology to enhance its service offering. The company purchased a Point-of-Sale service called Pulse, which allowed them to collect much higher-quality, real-time data about the entire value chain from the placing of the order to production to delivery. This data then allowed them to start customizing the product. For example, you can design your own pizza and you can monitor its progress as it is prepared, ready for delivery and then despatched. Domino's has also optimized the process of delivery – there are examples of people having a pizza delivered to them in their car while stuck in traffic. These innovative digital services have allowed Domino's to grow rapidly over the last five years or so, making them the clear leader in the home delivery pizza market.

These are classic examples of the ways you can bundle services around existing products in a way that creates value for the user and additional margin for the seller. It is always a useful exercise to ask colleagues to brainstorm the additional services you might offer and in particular to think about how advances in digital technology might enable those services.

#2. Outcome-Based Models. This is a more courageous leap into the unknown than the service-based approach. An outcome-based model says: 'I'm trying to figure out what it is that the customer really wants, even though they cannot articulate it.' As noted in the previous chapter, the handyman in the hardware store doesn't want a drill bit, he wants a hole in the wall. Outcome-based business models are a much bigger deal than service-based business models, by which we mean they are potentially more powerful if you can get them right, but also much more difficult because they take you out of your comfort zone and often into an entirely new world.

Here are a few examples. First, Pearson made a big play when John first became CEO for learning efficacy – in other words focusing on the outcome of education, not the inputs to it. The box below provides a detailed explanation of how this initiative worked.

Or consider the auto industry. Many people don't actually want to own a car, they simply want to be able to get from point A to point B as efficiently as possible, whenever they want to. This insight helped to make Uber the success it has become. Founder Travis Kalanick's original vision was that there will be so many Uber drivers on the road in a big city that no one would ever have any need to own a car again. It also led to the emergence of companies like DriveNow, created by BMW as a subscription-based service for people living in large cities, so that they had rapid access to a fleet of cars dotted around their neighbourhood.

Finally, there is the civil aerospace business. Rolls-Royce is one of the big three manufacturers of aircraft engines and was one of the pioneers of a 'power by the hour' business model. They used to simply sell their engines to the major airlines like British Airways or Delta but recognizing that the most important thing for an airline is a fully functioning and safe plane, they developed a commercial model with a fixed upfront element plus a variable element linked to how many hours their engines are used.

While attractive at a conceptual level, these outcome-based business models create huge uncertainty for the companies experimenting with them. Pearson generated significant intangible benefits from its learning efficacy programme and it played a role in its transition from ownership to more subscription type business models, but the influence has been more indirect and diffuse than the original vision. Rolls-Royce has benefited enormously from its power-by-the-hour business model, even though it struggled through the pandemic when planes were grounded. In contrast, BMW was not able to turn DriveNow into a commercial success on its own terms and has now turned it into a partnership with competitors.[3] Outcome-based models are generally high-risk/high-reward investments as they take you into a market space you do not fully understand, with new competitors and unpredictable margins. It is not always the case that you should jump into such opportunities – but it's always worth playing out what they might look like.

LEARNING EFFICACY: AN OUTCOME-BASED MODEL AT PEARSON

An early initiative from John on becoming CEO was to shift the focus in Pearson from education to learning, by emphasizing the outcomes it helped customers achieve. Thanks to the digital transition, it was becoming possible for the first time ever to track student engagement – for example in terms of the pages read and the time spent reading, and to measure progression, through formative quizzes and the like. It was also important for Pearson to take learning seriously as it was central to the company's mission. Pearson actually made a public commitment that within five years it would report externally on learning outcomes with the same rigour that it reported on financial results.

Of course, there was a lot of internal concern about how they might do this. Sales reps were saying, 'How are we going to sell this, what does this mean? If products are shown not to deliver better outcomes, even if they're popular with customers, would we stop selling them?' There was also external resistance, because in the world of education there are very few things one can achieve in isolation – Pearson could only achieve its goals through a partnership with teachers and policymakers. It proved to be a much more complicated and drawn-out process than anticipated.

Under John's leadership, Pearson put together a whole programme of activity around *learning efficacy*, working with the different divisions of Pearson to define the outcomes they were trying to achieve with their learners and how they would measure progress against those goals. The learning efficacy framework was also used to help with investment decisions. For example, a new product would not gain approval for launch unless there was a plan by which the outcome for learners would be enhanced. This started to fundamentally change the way people thought about product development, making it much more learning centric and accelerating the digital transformation of the company. In some of the new businesses the company started – working with universities to launch fully online degrees, running virtual schools, or learning a language online – commercial success followed only if students made good progress in their learning.

Pearson did report on learning outcomes in the annual report as promised, but actually it was the cultural change brought about within the company that was more important and the way in which it shifted business strategy. If you look at where Pearson now makes most of its money, it is not in content publishing but in learning and assessment, in enabling and certifying an outcome.

The Platform Perspective

The notion of a platform as a medium through which parties interact existed long before the internet came along. For example, the original 'marketplace' in a rural town was a platform – a place where farmers gathered to sell their produce to other townspeople. But the digital revolution has brought platforms into the mainstream. The reason they are so powerful is when they work well, they create value almost out of nothing – they bring together people who wanted to connect who could not do so before. And of course, there has been an explosion in the number and variety of platform businesses across the economy. The box below provides a bit more detail about the different ways these platforms make money.

HOW DO PLATFORMS MAKE MONEY?

All the big digital giants use platform-based business models to some degree. There are some who make physical products as well (notably Apple) but they all have platforms – connecting buyers and sellers – at the heart of their success. Broadly speaking, there are four ways platforms make money:

Fee for service. The last time you ordered an Uber, you paid a fee to the driver, but a percentage of that fee, of course, went to Uber. Last time you booked a hotel online through Expedia, Expedia took a share of that. It is a straightforward model – a fee for every time a service is used. What is interesting to look at is who gets charged because, of course, a platform is two-sided. In theory, a platform owner might charge both sides for access. In practice, one side is usually charged and the other side gets access to it for free.

Subscription-based model. If you have Netflix, for example, you pay a fee for the right to access the entire catalogue. If you pay that fee, you do not receive any advertising and you do not

---

pay every time you watch a movie. Likewise, Spotify charges a subscription fee for access to music. This is recurring and stable revenue for the platform, which is highly attractive. Amazon Prime is a variant of this, in that the subscription fee gives you access to a range of services, not just free movies.

Advertising. The *Guardian* newspaper does not charge a fee for their news. Its only predictable source of earnings is advertising. When you arrive at the *Guardian* website, you will typically see advertising closely related to your needs, thanks to some clever behind-the-scenes algorithms powered by Google. Advertising-based business models in the world of platforms are very common, particularly among smaller organizations. Small websites trying to get started will often use advertising as a (small) source of revenue.

Other uses of your data. Amazon's 'marketplace' offering allows third parties to sell products alongside Amazon's own inventory, creating an additional sources of data which Amazon can apply to its benefit in a host of different ways.

Many platform-based companies use several of these models at the same time. Spotify, for example, allows listening to music uninterrupted if you have paid the subscription model, or you can listen for free via the advertising-based model if you don't mind ads every few minutes in-between your songs. Twitter (X) pursues a primarily advertising-based business model, with no subscription or fee – although it has recently launched an opt-in paid, premium subscription service with reduced ads and additional features that could be helpful to people using the platform to market their own business.

Some companies do not have any discernible business model whatsoever – such as WhatsApp, owned by Meta. It is essentially cross-subsidized by Meta through the profits from Facebook.

Looking at the world from a platform perspective gives you new insights into your business model and how that business model might evolve. For example, before 1995 everyone thought of a newspaper as a product – a physical item that we paid money for. But we now know that a newspaper is a set of loosely related platforms. It is a medium for advertisers to reach customers, a medium for columnists to influence readers, a medium for buyers and sellers to interact (classified advertising), and so on. This insight led to the emergence of specialist classified advertisers, it changed the way we access journalistic insight and enabled the shift from print to digital advertising. The newspaper industry has changed beyond recognition compared to what it was like in the mid-1990s.

Here is how you can apply this platform perspective to your own business. Think about how competitors – and potential competitors – are encroaching on your space and making money. And then think about ways you can either forestall their advances or beat them at their own game. There are three primary tactics:

#1. **Aggregation.** This is where a platform company creates a comparison website or aggregator service, listing your service alongside everybody else's service and comparing them for the benefit of the end-user. For example, if you are a bank, your interest rates and your terms are listed alongside those of every other bank and then that information is updated continuously, allowing customers to cherry-pick who they want to borrow from.

If you find yourself being aggregated in this way, there is a huge risk of commoditization. You end up submitting to the terms of the aggregator and differentiation becomes almost impossible. We already talked earlier in this chapter about some of the options for fighting back against aggregation – for example, seeking to bypass the platform, increasing your bargaining power and finding innovative ways to rise above the threat of commoditization.

#2. **Disintermediation.** This is where the technology company, usually through the power of the internet, bypasses steps in an existing business system. The classic form of disintermediation is online shopping. The world simply doesn't need as many bricks-and-mortar retailers as it used to have because many consumers are comfortable with transacting online.

It is not only online shopping. There are also many industries out there where services are dramatically cheaper and delivered more efficiently through the power of technology. The threat of disintermediation is real and it may not be always possible to counter that threat. You must constantly remind customers why they used you in the first place and in many cases, you will have to accept that channels are no longer as valuable as they used to be.

#3. Unbundling. This refers to the separation out of different benefits or sources of value that used to be provided in a bundle. As noted above, the classic example is the newspaper – it reported news, it reported opinion, it had a lonely-hearts column, it had classified advertising and product and brand advertising as well. These were bundled together as a convenient way of giving a lot of value to the user. Of course, some of these features made a lot of money for newspapers, while other features did not.

With the advent of the internet, each of these features was separated out. Classified advertising, for example, makes no sense at all if you are trying to buy a car or a house when there is a website that does that job exclusively and at far greater volume and efficiency than any newspaper can. Newspapers have been dramatically unbundled. Many are struggling to survive.

How can you use these insights into technology-enabled business model innovation? The exercise in the box below is designed to summarize our ideas and to provoke a conversation in your company. Next time you have a strategy awayday, make copies and ask teams to think about the questions posed here.

BUSINESS MODEL INNOVATION EXERCISE

Where are the biggest opportunities for business model innovation in your industry? Here are five areas where there might be potential, though clearly some will be more relevant than others depending on your exact circumstances. Put your colleagues into small groups and ask them to find examples of possible innovations in each group. You should also ask ChatGPT for its suggestions, as if it were another group. Then pull everyone's ideas together and rank order the ideas in terms of their technical feasibility (can you do it?) and their economic viability (will it make money?).

1. Service-based models. What new services might you bundle in with your existing products or services to make them more attractive? How does digital technology enable these innovations?
2. Outcome-based models. What are your users actually buying? What could you do to shift your business model so that you addressed these fundamental needs?
3. Aggregation. How are your services currently being aggregated for users? Is there an opportunity for you to provide an aggregation service? Alternatively, what can you do to prevent aggregators from commoditizing your offerings?
4. Disintermediation. Is there a threat of disintermediation in your business? What can you do either to disintermediate others, or to avoid someone else disintermediating you?
5. Unbundling. Are there opportunities for you to unbundle someone else's business model and create a focused business in one profitable niche? Alternatively, what can you do to resist a new competitor unbundling your existing business?

LEADING THE PROCESS OF CHANGE – EXPERIMENTING WITH NEW BUSINESS MODELS

In the final part of this chapter, we shift the focus from what to how. Looking across the dozens of companies we have worked with in recent years, there is rarely a shortage of ideas about new business model ideas that might be launched but the process of turning those ideas into practice is where most companies get into difficulties.

Our guiding principle here is *learn, don't guess*. It's tempting to do the analysis, gain agreement on a course of action and then jump right in but as we discussed in the previous chapter, big bold moves often don't work out in a world of high uncertainty. A more experimental model typically pays dividends. Consider John's reflections first on how Pearson evolved its approach to innovation.

Within Pearson, there was a good level of discipline across the organization on spending on product development. We asked businesses some key questions: how much of what we spend is simply to sustain our existing investments? Are we spending on just upgrading or tweaking existing products or is investment more focused on high-risk, early-stage innovation?

When we first undertook this exercise, we discovered, not surprisingly, that most of our investments were not directed towards anything new. Now, there were very good reasons why – the risk return profile is very different for early-stage innovation compared to tweaking and iterating existing, proven products. However, just having the rigour of doing that and asking the questions honestly and openly gave us a real starting point.

Our next learning point, as we tried to shift more investment to earlier stage innovation, was making sure that we were not guessing or predetermining our results, but rather being open to learning along the way. We recognized that product development is very different in the digital world compared to the analogue world and therefore introducing the idea of a product manager and defining what that was, was a big learning point for us, especially as this was not a role that had existed previously. In the analogue world, our teams knew exactly what they were doing, could plan each edition cycle every three years and then hone each part to perfection, ready for release. In the digital world, it is completely different. You are iterating all the time. You try something, you get it in the hands of customers quickly, you receive the feedback and go again. These are skills and a culture that are difficult for a company to learn, and we knew we had to learn, fast.

We tried all sorts of things to try and create more of a learning or innovation culture. We got one of the founders of Google X, Tom Chi, to lead a day at our senior leadership retreat on rapid prototyping and then rolled it out through the whole company. We did three-day, company-wide innovation jams, involving thousands of colleagues in design thinking: tackling an initial big problem – an unmet customer need – and seeking collaborative solutions. We created a dedicated innovation and design hub at our corporate headquarters in London and New York, where we brought learners in to test early-stage products. We set aside a proportion of the annual budget to fund early-stage innovation and tried to free up time in people's day jobs to pursue it.

We acquired small, innovative, early-stage companies. Our biggest and earliest digital innovation – the creation of an online homework assessment platform – came from a small company spun out of MIT. Rather than licensing their technology, we bought the company, integrated it into our products and scaled it quickly. We made a concerted effort to replicate this success, with mixed results – because unless you can integrate an acquisition into the core capability of the company, and scale it, it is more likely to destroy value as it distracts your existing teams and doesn't allow the startup to focus either.

We became early-stage investors ourselves, partnering with an Edtech venture capital company called Learn Capital based out in San Mateo, in Silicon Valley, and taking small minority equity stakes in probably 100 or more early-stage startups. This hedged our bets – if a disruptive player proved successful, our investment would deliver a good return. More importantly, it gave us the chance to learn about what was happening in the wider ecosystem and access to a wide range of potential partners. The challenge was that, when these companies were very small, it was hard to get colleagues in Pearson to pay them much attention; by the time they started to scale and had our attention, the new companies were more sceptical and suspicious of our motives.

We formed our own Silicon Valley digital advisory network, drawing on the expertise of venture capital partners, Big Tech executives, entrepreneurs and academics, to test and challenge us. We brought in a lot of new digital talent. All of this helped us to increase our own pace of internal product innovation, to re-think our business models, to invest in the digital re-platforming of the company and to be much more learner and customer centric.

But I learnt two things. First, you've got to be careful not to succumb to 'innovation theatre', with a lot of activity and presentations, and everyone feeling better because we are talking about innovation. But are we actually doing anything productive? Are any fundamental changes occurring because of all the jams and exercises, the investments and the meetings? The second lesson is that when a company is really under extreme pressure from digital disruption – as we were – everybody is hoping against hope that with one innovation bound we can be free; that each new initiative will of itself solve all our problems. Of course, it doesn't work like that. As Pascal Finette, of Singularity University, would always remind me: for companies like Pearson, innovation is often about optimizing every single decision by a simple rubric: will it help us serve our customers better? By rigorously focusing on a seemingly endless list of things right in front of you, you amass a huge amount of incremental change that over time is what makes the difference. This is the alchemy of innovation, if you like. It's not one thing, it's everything. It takes time, but it works, and it builds on the huge market, product and customer knowledge and insights that incumbents like Pearson already have.

Pearson's approach to innovation will be familiar to executives in many established companies. In particular, the idea of opening up to startups and external sources of ideas, rather than relying entirely on your own internal R&D, is one that has become very widespread in recent years. This is not to say it always works, because the truth is that all approaches to innovation have inherently low yields but it is a good way of tilting the odds in your favour.

The other aspect of Pearson's approach that is noteworthy is the cultivation of an experimental mindset. We will say more about this later in the book, but for now it is useful to flesh out exactly what we mean by experimentation.

An experiment is a conscious action taken to test a hypothesis – for example, if we do X then Y will happen. We monitor X and Y and we either gain support for a hypothesis or we do not. Regardless of the outcome, we have learnt something useful and this informs our next step.

This notion of experimentation applies to any sort of scientific work. In the business world, it is useful to separate out two types of activity. The first is what digital marketers called 'A/B testing' and it has become *de rigueur* as a way of improving the effectiveness of online advertising. The marketer might take an ad for a burger and fries at McDonald's and then tweak it slightly, putting a different image of the burger or changing the background colour. The two ads then run side by side, with half the viewers seeing one and half the other. The outcome, typically the click-through rate for the ad, is then monitored carefully and with a large enough sample it is possible to end up with clear evidence that one ad is more effective than the other. It is a classic form of experiment – we change one thing, we monitor what happens and we adapt. Almost every website these days has been fine-tuned through a series of these A/B experiments.

The second and more interesting type can be thought of as business experiments, where we consciously try out some new service or business model to see if it has any potential. Clearly this type of experiment cannot be done as clinically as the A/B testing described above but we can undertake a less rigorous approach by trying out something new within a controlled segment and with a clear if/then hypothesis in mind. We have seen many companies be quite creative in trying out new business ideas in this way.

Here is one example that Julian was responsible for at London Business School (LBS). When the school first considered online learning, around six or seven years ago, no one knew know if online learning products would be any good, so they ran an experiment.

They offered a few courses online using their own marketing machinery and at a price point of around £1,500. They developed and offered others through a partner company called Emeritus at a similar price point, using their marketing and tapping into their global reach. LBS also offered a few through a very large platform called Coursera, which had a much lower price point (roughly £50 at that point, for someone who wanted to earn a certificate), but with no live learning elements. The point is that because they did not know whether online courses would sell or not, they deliberately offered these three different options and tracked the results very carefully. How did it work out? For a while, the courses offered through Emeritus did very well, but over time, LBS concluded that selling their online courses directly was the best option.

In short, running experiments like this are the best way to move from concept to working prototype and ultimately a commercial endeavour. Remember that is still at the fairly early stages of any business model innovation. At some point, if the experiment works, there is a conversation to be had about scaling it up rapidly, a topic we discuss in more detail in Chapter 4.

SUMMARY OF CHAPTER

The most important change in the business landscape over the last 15 years has been the emergence of the big digital-platform companies, from Amazon and Alphabet through to Uber and Netflix. These companies have become extremely powerful and have reshaped many parts of the business landscape.

For the big incumbent companies with strong legacy interests, this transition has been challenging and inspiring in equal measure. It's challenging because in many cases these digital platform companies have seen an opportunity that incumbents either didn't see or were not able to capitalize on and built much more powerful and profitable companies. It's inspiring because digital technology more generally – and the new platforms being built specifically – is suddenly opening up a wealth of new opportunities for value creation, many of which incumbents are best placed to seize. As we have shown over the course of this chapter, there are plenty of new angles available for business model innovation. What is needed is a creative spirit to identify these angles and then an experimental way of working that allows you to put some of your ideas into practice.

Of course, none of this is easy to do. It requires a rethinking of how you make decisions and empower people to take risks, and often needs wholesale changes to the basic structures through which your company operates. In the next chapter we will look at some of the new ways of working that are made possible by the digital revolution.

4

Digital Ways of Working: From Agile to Virtual

Most large incumbent companies are organized with a high degree of hierarchy, a function of both their size and their age. An important but often overlooked role of hierarchy during the industrial era was for the transmission of information. It was an effective way of pushing orders down through the chain and for aggregating data back up to the top. Indeed, one prominent theory of organizations back in the 1970s was to view them as 'information processing systems'.[1] This is why the digital revolution is so important to how organizations function and why it enables us to think much more creatively about how we work. The passing of information up and down the hierarchy is no longer a constraint. Some managers may still choose to be a bit secretive, but there is no technical obstacle to sharing information on a company-wide basis and there are potentially enormous benefits to doing so.

In this chapter we take a close look at the implications of ubiquitous information for how we work, with a particular interest on the emergence of less hierarchical and less bureaucratic models. We start with John's experience as CEO of Pearson, then focus on some of the new ways of thinking about structure, culture and mindset in today's organizations.

THE COST OF COMPLEXITY

One of the issues John grappled with at Pearson was how best to organize the company. When he first joined Pearson in 1997, it was essentially still a conglomerate with a small head office. The role of the head office was an important but relatively narrow one. It decided what businesses should be in the portfolio, what companies to buy and sell, and who the CEOs of each business should be. It agreed the financial plans of the portfolio companies and managed relationships with shareholders. Pretty much everything else was done within each portfolio company.

However, over the next 15 years, Pearson's portfolio of companies changed very significantly. The businesses that Pearson owned in television, theme parks, investment banking, financial information, data and magazine publishing were all sold. This came hard on the heels of businesses in fine wine, fine dining, regional newspapers, even avocado farming, that had been sold only a few years earlier. Within a few years, Penguin and the *Financial Times* would be divested as well.

Over this 15-year period, Pearson bought some 50 different education-related businesses of varying sizes in countries all over the world. As the Pearson portfolio became more focused on a single field of activity, the role of the head office started to change. It became more activist, playing a bigger role in areas like talent management and technology. Various efforts were made to encourage greater collaboration across the company. However, there was still a strong vestige of a conglomerate culture and tensions grew between what should be done at the centre and what should be done at the operating company level. For example, if the centre felt an operating company was not moving quickly enough on the digital front, it would invest in a separate operation. When the centre tried to roll out a piece of back-office technology company-wide, it would sometimes meet major resistance from one or more businesses within the portfolio. It was then often forced to back off, but not before spending time and often a lot of money on the doomed initiative.

This led to a growing belief around the board table that the time was ripe for a fundamental change in the way the company was run.

There were non-executive directors who had worked in large global companies run along the lines of a matrix. They voiced the widely shared concern that acquiring all these new education companies had brought size and complexity, but not necessarily any real economies of scale. The data bore out these concerns. Pearson had 63 unique enterprise resource planning (ERP) systems, 120 different ways of creating content and hundreds of product platforms. Online, there were 150 storefronts, 17,000 domains, 3,000 unique websites, 40 different instances of Salesforce, 93 data centres, only 5 per cent of which were in the public Cloud, and we had the equivalent of 6,200 people working full-time on technology, which was a lot for a company of our size. The people director had counted at least 15 people in the company with the title of chief technology officer.

Did any of this matter? Well, when Pearson was a conglomerate with a portfolio of stand-alone businesses with no synergies or economies of scale, probably not. However, Pearson now aspired to be the world's leading education company. John's view was there were synergies and economies of scale to be had from running the company on shared platforms.

The growth and profit engine of the company was the US college publishing business whose very high levels of profitability in effect cross-subsidized the rest of the company. That meant that if the underlying profitability of the rest of the company was not improved, problems would be stored up for the future. Every part of Pearson had big digital aspirations. Herein lay the next problem: if each portfolio business invested in its own digital re-platforming, then the cost would be astronomical and the company would end up replicating the inefficient, complex and redundant way of running its analogue businesses in the digital world. In an analogue world, duplication and redundancy is frustrating but rarely fatal financially; in a digital world, it is prohibitively expensive. In sum, Pearson's challenge, like so many other large firms, was an overly complex organization that had evolved over time, with multiple inefficiencies and slow in its decision-making. This problem needed resolving fast if Pearson were to succeed as a digital first company.

REORGANIZING FOR CLARITY AND SIMPLICITY

Faced with an overly complex structure, one of the first things John decided was to initiate the biggest change in the way the company was run, possibly in its 175-year history. He decided to run Pearson as a more integrated global operating company, with fully integrated functions in finance, HR, technology, corporate affairs and legal, each of which reported to a single global head. Here is his reflection on the process:

We created a new product organization to oversee all research in product development globally, organized along several industry verticals. This helped in two ways. Firstly, in ensuring our commitment to efficacy and secondly, that all our new products were highly learner-centric and focused entirely on the outcomes for the customer. All our sales and operations were then aligned through customer-centric geographies. We also mapped out for the first time how the company was run and what our target operating model should be. We took great care to work through for each scenario who was responsible, who was accountable, who had the right to be consulted and who had the right to be informed. We did not treat every part of the company the same and in the parts of the company where we saw no immediate revenue synergies, we created what we called integrated businesses combining product and sales.

We kickstarted this organizational review involving the 200 or so most senior leaders, alongside the strategy refresh in Autumn 2012, within weeks of John being appointed CEO. We then announced and implemented the new organizational approach a year later. We had kept the whole company involved and informed about the review as we went through the process. Even so, we grossly underestimated the scale of the change. It required virtually every job in the company to be remapped to the new target operating model, causing immense anxiety and concern. The new organization required huge changes in our ways of working, styles of leadership, behaviour, culture. There were valid questions about the new organizational design that we grappled with intensely for long periods of time. We were internally focused at a time when externally our markets were starting to change quite quickly. Were we still too hierarchical with too much power now resting in the centre? Was decision-making in the matrix style of working too bureaucratic and slowing the company down when it needed to move quickly? Was separating product and sales organizationally the right move? Did it risk diluting the power of customer insights and reducing the urgency with which we could launch new products to market? In organizing technology to maximize economies of scale, were we blunting innovation and by running finance, HR, etc. as global functions, were we denying P&L managers the ability to reduce cost quickly in response to changing market conditions or competitive performance?

We did not dismiss or deny any of these challenges. Instead, the organization design continued to evolve and change as we wrestled them and as the analogue to digital transformation in our markets gathered pace.

While there were challenges, the organizational changes enabled the radical re-platforming of the company that was vital to its digital transformation. By 2020, the company ran on one Cloud-based enterprise resource planning system. There was now one modern streamlined digital first workflow, delivering digital native mobile first products to market 50 per cent faster than previously, with one global learning platform. There was one global implementation of Salesforce, one unified e-commerce solution and a mobile optimized Web presence. There were only five data centres remaining, with 95 per cent of the company's operations now in the Cloud. Over 70 per cent of Pearson's sales were digital, compared to around 25 per cent eight years earlier. We employed 70 per cent fewer technology stuff, 1,900 compared to the previous 6,200. Across the company, we reduced the cost base in real terms by over 25 per cent, saving over 1 billion pounds annually and moving the company from one of the least to one of the most efficient of its peers, with further savings to flow over the next few years.

A NEVER-ENDING PROCESS OF CHANGE

Looking back, we can see that the radical changes made to the way Pearson was run brought its own set of challenges – but that the company would not have been able to survive the digital transformation and be as well-placed now to prosper in the future, had John not instigated the changes described here. We can draw two wider lessons from this story – organizations need to evolve continually and any organizational design requires trade-offs.

You sometimes hear people complaining that you are making changes in the organization that are effectively reversing changes made only a few years earlier, as if that suggests your earlier changes were wrong. It is understandable why colleagues working in a specific part of the company get fed up with what they perceive to be too much unnecessary organizational change ('change fatigue')[2] that just gets in the way of them doing their job. As a leader, you need to be sensitive to these concerns, but that shouldn't stop you from making changes when necessary, even if it means unwinding something you'd implemented only a few years earlier. For the truth is that in many companies going through a major transformation, a back-and-forth between a period of greater centralization followed swiftly by a greater emphasis on decentralization may be exactly what you need.

Pearson's organizational design has continued to evolve again since John left the company. It is now run as five integrated global business units (GBU), with shared expertise and capabilities around digital and direct-to-consumer but with each of the GBU leaders having full P&L responsibility. In many ways, it is now largely run as we envisaged the company should be back in 2012, but it would have been too big a leap to go from where we were then straight to the way the company is organized now. There were many issues that needed to be addressed first.

And, inevitably, the new organizational design will bring a fresh set of challenges. For example, each of the five global business units operates in the UK. This means five independent sales teams, each maximizing sales of their own products, often selling to the same

institutional customers. Education is a highly politicized environment in which to do business, with multiple stakeholders and
overlapping regulatory and political concerns. If not co-ordinated,
the actions that one part of the company takes to maximize sales
could damage the prospects of another. So, should each GBU operate in the UK independently of each other, completely focused on
maximizing their own performance? Or should they work together
to build deeper relationships with the biggest institutional customers
and manage regulatory and reputational risks? The answer, of course,
is that they should be doing both, but it is almost impossible to design
an organization that aligns and motivates people to do both equally
well. So, what happens is that you organize to emphasize one for a
while, then switch to the other and then switch back again

The major lesson from all this is that there is no one right way to
run a company. Context and timing are everything. Trade-offs need
to be made constantly. In any organization, decisions get made and
things get done, as Niall Ferguson describes it in his book, *The Tower
and the Square: Networks, Hierarchies and the Struggle for Global
Power*,[3] through a mixture of hierarchy and networks, some of those
networks are formal, others less so.

Some tasks – like the radical re-platforming of a major analogue
conglomerate to survive and prosper in the digital world – require,
at least for a period, a degree of hierarchy. Other tasks – like inno-
vating around new product and business models to capitalize on that
re-platforming and grow in a platform dominated ecosystem – lend
themselves best to a more devolved, networked organization. It's not
that one is right and the other wrong, you'll always need elements of
both. It's about ensuring you understand the benefits and downsides
with both approaches and are constantly evolving your organization, adjusting the balance of power between the hierarchy and the
network, to reflect the changing needs of your customers and your
markets.

Here is another perspective on structural change. After he left BT
Group in 2018, Gavin Patterson took up a new role as chief revenue
officer of Salesforce. His experiences largely align with John's. This

is Gavin comparing the functional organization design of Salesforce with the divisional structure of BT:

Salesforce is organized on a functional basis. When I was the chief revenue officer, it was a sales and distribution job. I contributed to the overall direction as part of the leadership team. But in spite of being on that leadership team, I had a functional role. Everybody has a functional role. The beauty of that is you can move really quickly in terms of making changes in the market, moving investment around. It also ensures that you remain very disciplined as to why you are in business together. There is only a single P&L and that's what drives product development, the sales process, investment.

From my own experience, and looking at many different companies within a sector, the more divisionally oriented your business is, the more difficult it is to get things done on a group wide basis, because the budgets, the profits, the power sit at a divisional level and it's very difficult to get people to work across the business. At BT, this made it much harder to drive pan group transformation projects. You begin to question why you're in business together if there aren't shared assets, shared capabilities.

Too often, things are delegated down to give people in divisional jobs some 'general management' experience. But in reality, you lose synergy, you lose agility and you lose an ability to invest. A functional model where you really clean up the business so that the management team have a shared set of incentives, metrics and they each play a specific role towards those rather than having two IT organizations, one in the division and one centrally, makes a huge difference because that allows you to move quickly. If you retain a functional model as long as possible, I think you can move the business far more. You can be far more agile and you can create commonality. You can create investment cases. You can take a long-term view and you can drive change.

Of course, the functional approach that Gavin ascribes works less well in a portfolio-type company, with a range of different product, and business models that have less in common. The general point here stands: there is no one best way of organizing a large company but the capacity to adapt to changing circumstances – to stay agile – is of vital importance in today's fast-changing business world.

BUREAUCRATIC CREEP

Pearson's story of transformation is one many will recognize. Let's now abstract from it to look at the broader principles of organization structure and how digital technology changes what's possible for large incumbent companies.

The starting point for a conversation about new ways of working is bureaucracy – co-ordination through standardized rules and procedures. The term was introduced by German sociologist Max Weber, who saw bureaucracy as an effective way of structuring large-scale industrial activities because it encouraged specialization and reduced waste. It also reduced the risk of corruption and cronyism. But the term has become tainted over the years and is typically viewed in a pejorative light in the business world today. Here's an example from an internet chat: 'The successful bureaucrat understands that acting is risky. There should never, ever be any urgency to act and the objective should be to delay getting anything done.'[4] While this is a slightly facetious way of thinking about bureaucracy, it captures a real truth, which is that bureaucracy in its pure form is highly risk-averse; it is designed to ensure that nothing goes wrong but also that really nothing very much changes either. Bureaucracy has other related side effects as well. It is slow-moving and somewhat immune to external forces for change. And it is debilitating for the individuals within the system, in that it requires them to follow rules, whether those rules make sense or not. Innovation and creativity are driven out.

Here is a piece of data from Gary Hamel, a Visiting Professor at London Business School. He has collected data looking at the number of people in different roles and professions. The data is from the US, but the same story applies in many other countries. From 1983 to the present day, there has been a doubling in the number of people in the entire US workforce with jobs as managers and administrators, whereas the number in value-adding roles, those doing the work, such as the technical people or salespeople, the research scientists and so forth, has only grown by 44 per cent over the same period. Bureaucracy, defined in terms of administrators overseeing the actual day-to-day work of people doing the work, has grown much, much quicker.[5]

Why don't we see more progress in how large organizations operate? Many companies try to simplify and reduce layers of hierarchy, make themselves faster and more customer-centric yet we don't see much evidence of improvement. Part of the reason is there are contradictory pressures at work in any organization. Pressures from the market put a premium on speed, clarity and simplicity, thereby encouraging the types of delayering and empowering activities Pearson went through while John was CEO.

But at the same time there are strong inertial pressures. Some of these come from regulators. Whenever an industry attracts regulatory scrutiny because of an accident or error, it ends up with more burdensome rules. We have seen this a lot in financial services, but it also applies to media, pharmaceuticals and other sectors. Whenever there is a downturn, or a company comes under financial pressure, it is human nature to pull control back, closer to the centre, to ensure all the right actions are being taken to get the company back on track. As a result, you see companies moving towards greater degrees of empowerment and freedom, and then once a shock happens, they swing back to being more centralized again. There have been many companies over the past few years, who have gone through this pendulum swing of more and less freedom over the years. That is part of the natural course of things. It also explains to some degree why we have not seen anything like as much progress as we would anticipate.

But here is the point, and it is central to the thesis of this book. Thanks to information technology, some of the transformations of organizations that have long been dreamt of but not remotely achieved may finally be realized. The digital revolution has allowed the sharing of information across the organization both laterally and vertically, in unprecedented ways, making it possible to empower and delegate in ways not seen before.

DIGITAL WAYS OF WORKING

Since the internet revolution in the mid-1990s, we have seen a blossoming of the availability and the quality of information available to us in our daily lives and within our organizations. Pre-internet, it was possible for centralized computers to share information widely onto PCs and desktops through corporate networks but with the advent of the World Wide Web, it became possible for anyone to access information from more or less any computer in the world (subject to permission protocols, of course).

What this means in terms of how organizations function is that, suddenly, we can work in vastly different ways than before. Thanks to technology, we can now share information vertically and horizontally in real time with anyone, through channels such as Slack, Teams, Zoom, Facebook and many more. That is a huge dramatic change, which makes it possible to organize and do things radically differently. Virtual working is also possible. In bygone days, we all had to sit in the same stuffy office building because that was how we would communicate with each other. Thanks to digital technology, we can now work anywhere and have almost the same quality of conversations as before (though we lose a sense of community – a point we return to later in the chapter).

The digital revolution has created a template for change. In other words, it is more than just a set of technologies that enable; rather it gives us clues as to what sharing looks like. If you take the classic shift from mainframe computers to personal computers to Cloud computing (discussed in detail in Chapter 5, *see also* page 105), that exactly tracks the way our thinking about organizing has evolved – from traditional top-down to more delegated in the world of the PC, and now towards much more sharing in collaborative, agile teams with very little hierarchical involvement at all. In the remainder of this chapter, we discuss this shift in three specific ways: changes in how we organize work (structure), changes in how we think and behave (mindset) and changes in where and when we work (the virtual workplace).

CHANGES IN HOW WE ORGANIZE WORK: INTRODUCING MANAGEMENT MODELS

Here is a simple framework to help you think about organizing in a digital world, first developed in Julian's earlier book with Jonas Ridderstrale, *Fast/Forward*.[6] There are three generic management models: bureaucracy, meritocracy and adhocracy. We have already talked about **bureaucracy** as co-ordination through standardized rules and procedures and through hierarchical oversight. Government departments and large manufacturing operations are typical settings for bureaucracy.

Meritocracy is an organizing model built around knowledge and expertise that privileges an individual's knowledge as more important than their formal position within a system. In a meritocracy, we are saying we want to ensure that the collective knowledge of the organization, often dispersed across many individuals and teams, is brought to bear so that when there is a problem or an issue, we can address it and solve it in the right way. Professional services firms and academic departments in universities operate on a meritocratic basis.

Adhocracy is an organizing model built around action, in other words privileging doing ahead of the discussing (meritocracy) or following rules (bureaucracy). If we think of examples, the classic form of adhocracy is a startup, a small company with maybe 10 or 20 employees with no formal structures at all. The most important thing – the only thing – that matters in a startup is getting things done, finding a way to sell a product or service to a customer. There's a lot of hustle, experimentation, trying new things and converting ideas into action.

These are three generic organizing models. While a lot of the language around adhocracy is positive in tone, we are not saying 'bureaucracy bad, adhocracy good' – that would be too simplistic. Rather, the argument is that each of these models has its place. For example, if you work in a nuclear power plant, you need bureaucracy as human lives are at stake; people need to follow rules for operating under certain circumstances. If you work in a science lab, meritocracy is likely the dominant model because you are trying to solve difficult problems and advance science. If you work in a startup, or in the more customer-focused parts of a larger organization such as in sales or business development, you need an adhocracy.

In fact, the chances are your organization is a combination of these three different models. The question to ask is therefore what is the right mix of models for your specific circumstances? We have included a little exercise (see the box below) to help you think about which model is currently dominant and which you might think of using in the future.

MANAGEMENT MODEL EXERCISE

1. Consider the organization where you work. If it is a large organization, focus on the specific business unit or operation where you work.

2. Answer the six questions below, by indicating the extent to which each situation is managed through bureaucracy, meritocracy or adhocracy. You should circle a number in each of the three columns for each question.

3. Add up the six numbers to give you an overall measure of the extent to which each of the three models is present in your organization. Don't be surprised if you end up with two of the three equally strong – many organizations are in fact a combination of models.

4. Having done this analysis, it's often useful to discuss it with a colleague and ask yourself: does this seem to be a desirable model (or combination of models) for our business right now? And if not, what steps might be taken to shift towards a more desirable model (or combination)?

Circle one number for each:
5=always, 4=usually, 3=often,
2=sometimes, 1=rarely, 0=never

	BUREAUCRACY	MERITOCRACY	ADHOCRACY
COORDINATION	**By Rules**	**Mutual Adjustment**	**Around Opportunity**
Question 1. Your company is exploring a strategic alliance with an important supplier or customer. Which of the following approaches do people gravitate to?	We have a very structured approach, we are cautious about the risks involved, and we pay a lot of attention to the legal contracts (5 4 3 2 1 0)	We spend a lot of time getting to know the other party, to see if there are complementarities, and to see how well we can work with them. (5 4 3 2 1 0)	We start very informally, trying out something low-risk quite quickly, and building up from there. (5 4 3 2 1 0)
Question 2. You are seeking to get various functions or business units to align around a complex project. how do you proceed?	We define clear deliverables at the outset, and we make sure everyone knows who is accountable and what their roles are. We monitor progress against these deliverables. (5 4 3 2 1 0)	We bring key people from the various functions together, we spend time discussing our respective roles and how we can all contribute. We meet periodically and we adjust depending on how things are going (5 4 3 2 1 0)	We work closely with the end user or customer for the project, and we provide frequent updates to them; project meetings are frequent, and often involve significant changes depending on user feedback. (5 4 3 2 1 0)
DECISION-MAKING	**Hierarchy**	**Logical Argument**	**Iteration/experiment**
Question 3. A front-line employee is dealing with an unhappy customer, who feels the service the company has provided hasn't been as good as expected. How does the typically respond?	She pushes back, explaining that the company acted in accordance with its formal policies. If the customer pushes harder, she escalates the problem to her boss. (5 4 3 2 1 0)	She seeks to understand what went wrong – to get to the bottom of the problem, so that the system can be improved in the future. (5 4 3 2 1 0)	She realizes the customer is upset, and takes immediate action to pacate him, sometimes even overturning formal policy (5 4 3 2 1 0)
Question 4. There is a request from a business unit or team for some additional funds (a further 5%-10% over the allocated amount) to invest in what they say is an important new project. How does their boss respond?	He says no. There is a well-established process for requesting funds; wait until next year. (5 4 3 2 1 0)	He asks for more information: What is the business case? Why does this merit special consideration? Depending on these answers, he may make an exception. (5 4 3 2 1 0)	He tries to help the operating unit by providing a small amount of money, so they can test out their idea with limited funding, and then ask for more money later. (5 4 3 2 1 0)
MOTIVATION	**Extrinsic Rewards**	**Personal Mastery**	**Achievement**
Question 5. Where do your senior executives prefer to spend their time?	At their desks, chairing reviews and board meetings, seeking input from direct reports. (5 4 3 2 1 0)	Debating strategic issues with colleagues, reading up on the latest thinking, in the lab or taking to experts about developments in the industry. (5 4 3 2 1 0)	Out in the field meeting with customers and prospective customers, walking the corridor, talking to front-line employees about their challenges. (5 4 3 2 1 0)
Question 6. What is the primary source of motivation and job-satisfaction for mid-level employees?	Getting well paid for their work, getting a bonus for delivering on goals, getting promoted (5 4 3 2 1 0)	Doing a high-quality piece of work, being recognized as an expert in an important area, working with smart colleagues (5 4 3 2 1 0)	Making things happen, meeting difficult deadlines, being recognized for delivering creative or surprising results (5 4 3 2 1 0)
	Total score for bureaucracy: ___	Total score for meritocracy: ___	Total score for adhocracy: ___

92

We have used this exercise with many executives in different companies and sectors around the world. Those who work for a large company typically operate with a combination of bureaucracy and meritocracy as the dominant models. And they typically note that they would like a bit more adhocracy, given the need for greater speed and responsiveness in their industry.

Our observation is that you need to actively carve out or protect those activities that need to be managed through adhocracy, because if you do not, you will be pulled back into one of the other models. To illustrate, consider a hypothetical meeting where somebody says, *'We need to act now. This is an opportunity that's really important. If we don't act soon, we're going to lose out to our competitors.'* This is an adhocracy-based argument. Somebody else says, *'Let's check with the lawyers or compliance first,'* which is the bureaucracy talking, finding ways of slowing things down. Then there are others saying, *'That's a good idea, but we have not thought it through. We need to step back. We need to make sure we gather all the relevant people together to discuss it to make sure that everybody is comfortable with this way forward.'* And that is the meritocracy talking, people who delight in having endless conversations. The point is, these three models aren't just a way of structuring work, they are a way of looking at the world. And the bureaucratic and meritocratic outlooks, in their own particular ways, tend to slow things down.

Adhocracy in Born-Digital Companies

To give you a glimmer of what's possible in terms of organizing model, here are some examples of what adhocracy looks like in 'born-digital' companies, those founded during or after the internet revolution, where the founders and leaders see the world through a digital lens. These companies have no legacy infrastructure problems, no old assets that must be reconfigured. They start small and grow fast from that base, which gives them a head start in terms of thinking differently. Indeed, they often have this slightly irreverent attitude to traditional ways of thinking about things. Mark Zuckerberg's original Facebook mantra of *'move fast and break things'* is a mindset shared by many Silicon Valley companies, who don't just want to create novel revolutionary products, but also want to think very differently about how we work.

Google's purpose is to organize the world's information to make it universally accessible and useful. Founders Larry Page and Sergey Brin sought to do this by being revolutionary. Rather than make things work 10 per cent better than before, they wanted to make them work 10 times better (in other words, 1,000 per cent). To do this, they sought to make work as fluid and non-bureaucratic as before. One practice they created was *innovation time off*. If you were an engineer in the early days, you could spend up to 20 per cent of your time (i.e. one whole day in the week) working on your own pet projects, things which no one had sanctioned because they seemed like an interesting thing to do. Google also had a concept 70/20/10, the idea that resources should be allocated roughly 70 per cent towards today's money-making activities, 20 per cent towards tomorrow's money-makers and 10 per cent towards 'day after tomorrow' projects, those with a very long horizon. Google X is the name they gave to the unit where all these '10X' projects were originally hot-housed – for example, Project Loon (using hot-air balloons to provide internet access in places without infrastructure) and the original driverless car project.

Spotify, the Stockholm-based music streaming company, was perhaps the first to take the notion of agile self-organized teams, as first used in software development, and to scale it up to their entire organization. Agile has become the most popular workplace innovation of the last 15 years, because it gives employees the opportunity to shape their own daily tasks, operate on their own schedule and work more closely with users to ensure that they are providing a product or service that users actually want. Spotify helped to spread the word on this new model, thanks in no small measure to a famous YouTube video on Spotify's 'engineering culture' by Henrik Kniberg.[7] Many companies, such as ING below, have taken Spotify's ideas about squads, tribes and chapters to heart.

Valve is a Seattle-based gaming company famous for products like Half-Life and the Steam portal. Founded by Gabe Newell, an ex-Microsoft executive, Valve has around 400 employees but no managers. Newell decided to take to extremes the notion that we do not need structure to create co-ordinated action. Once a new employee is hired at Valve (and the selection process is highly rigorous), they are free to figure out for themselves what jobs to work on. It sounds chaotic, and to some degree it is, but, perhaps inevitably, an informal structure has taken shape over the years to facilitate co-ordination.

Adhocracy Within Established Firms
How does the principle of adhocracy apply to established firms? We are not advocating blowing up the structures of big established companies and removing all managers. That will not happen and for very good reasons. However, we see a lot of value in extracting some of the principles that we see in born digitals and applying them in a sensible way to big established companies.

Let's consider a few examples, starting with the well-known case of ING Group and its pioneering work ten years ago in restructuring its head office on agile principles.

ING Group was formed in 1991 through the merger of three Dutch financial firms. It was hit badly by the global financial crisis in 2008 and went through a consolidation and cost-cutting process in the years following, including an initiative called 'Less is More', which was designed to streamline its operational processes. As part of the company's 'think forward' initiative put in place by incoming CEO Ralph Hamers, a project looking at the future of retail banking was started by Bart Schlatmann, the Dutch COO. This project focused on the way customer demands were changing and on the desire from inside the bank to operate in a less bureaucratic way. Bart and his team sought inspiration from several born-digital companies, including visiting Spotify in Stockholm, and they alighted on 'agile working' as a way to make the bank more customer-focused and more efficient at the same time. The change initiative was launched in 2015 with the name RIO ('Redesign Into Omnichannel'). The old hierarchical structure was thrown out and replaced with around 350 self-organized 'squads' clustered into 14 'tribes' with several cross-cutting 'chapters' that provided specialized expertise in key areas.

There was inevitable concern about this new model from some quarters, including the employees' Works Council, some in the parent company and the European Central Bank, but Bart and his team had sufficient credibility, thanks to earlier cost-cutting programmes, that they were able to bring everyone on board.

How did this agile transformation work out? Overall, it was a clear success story, with improvements in employee engagement, customer satisfaction and cost efficiency within two years. Taking a longer view, ING Bank has continued to perform well, though gradually, as senior executives moved on and others took over, some of the internal structures have gravitated back towards more traditional ways of working. The cadre of 'agile coaches' who were an important part of the original design, for example, was disbanded in the early 2020s.

Many observers continued to be surprised and impressed by the scale of the organizational change ING put in place, especially given the highly regulated banking environment in which they were operating. We would argue there were three contributory factors. First, Bart and his team did a lot of work in advance, building the case to try something different and with a lot of credibility from having done earlier re-engineering projects. Second, they had a CEO, Ralph Hamers, who was prepared to take risks. ING itself had quite a legacy of being creative and innovative within its industry and the CEO was able to link back to this history. Third, there was also a genuine openness from those at the top to give up a lot of their traditional formal authority. Indeed, the Spotify executives they visited in Stockholm asked them at one point, 'We see you like this model, but how much are you prepared to give up?' The mental shift the senior team had to go through, to realize they were no longer in control in the traditional way, was huge and a necessary element to make it work.

Many other firms have looked at what ING Bank has done and tried to copy it, but with mixed levels of success. Some lacked the necessary preconditions, or rushed the process, or were operating in a very different cultural environment. Our observation would be that you should always handle these case studies of organizational change with caution. Any change programme is not only risky but will take a long time. You must be prepared to be in these things for the long haul, for at least three to five years before you can be confident that you are achieving success. While new ways of working can be very effective, it takes a lot of time and a lot of competence to put them in place.

While ING was unusual in the extent of its appetite for innovative ways of working, it is by no means alone. A couple of other examples. One is the French energy company **Engie**. In the mid-2010s, its energy markets division, one of the more entrepreneurial parts of the organization, adopted the organizing model called Holacracy. This is a highly decentralized way of working, invented by management thinker Brian Robertson, whereby self-organizing 'circles' of employees define their own priorities and their own mode of co-ordination with adjacent circles. We won't describe the details here for space reasons[8] and, in any case, it is conceptually like the agile model that ING put in place. Engie's energy market division got some real benefits from its foray into Holacracy, including improvements in financial performance and internal engagement. However, the Holacracy model *per se* was gradually scaled back after its initial implementation and the way of working returned to something that employees were more comfortable with.

Another interesting case study is **Bayer**, the large German life and plant sciences company. Under incoming CEO, Bill Anderson, Bayer instituted a model called 'dynamic shared ownership' (DSO), described in a press release in January 2024 as follows:

> *It will reduce hierarchies, eliminate bureaucracy, streamline structures and accelerate decision-making processes. The aim of the new operating model is to make the company much more agile and significantly improve its operational performance.*

Like ING Group, Bayer took a 'big-bang' approach to its change programme, with large numbers of people across the company involved – around 170 teams and 4,000 people as of March 2024. The focus also seems to be on empowering customer-facing teams so they can be more responsive and decisive, and in shifting the roles of leaders. According to Heike Prinz, Chief Talent Officer,

> *A key prerequisite is shifting leaders from managers that command and control to visionaries that guide teams in defining the outcomes to deliver on our mission; from planners to architects that shape a value-creating system; from directors to catalysts that remove roadblocks; and from controllers to coaches that help teams learn and build the capabilities needed.*[9]

The new model was launched in autumn 2023 so at the time of writing, it is too early to say how successful DSO might be for Bayer. They reported some dramatic improvements in decision-making speed (for example, a consumer health team in Asia moved launch dates forward by six months, shortening internal processes by 60 per cent and resulting in a 30 per cent increase in value), but they also committed to not making any compulsory redundancies before 2026 to bring the labour unions on board with the plan.

These three examples are illustrative of the challenges and opportunities large incumbent companies face as they seek to embrace digital ways of working. It is hard work – two steps forward, one step back – and yet it is also an essential part of staying relevant in a fast-changing world.

CHANGES IN HOW WE THINK AND BEHAVE: DIGITAL MINDSET

Let's shift our attention from structure to culture and mindset – from the formal lines of activity to the informal way of working. This too has been significantly affected by the digital revolution. For example, a 35-year-old who has always worked for Google is going to have a very different mindset than a 60-year old who grew up in the pre-digital era. We use the term 'mindset' simply to refer to how people look at the world and the assumptions they make about why things operate the way they do. Mindset then shapes individual behaviour, though obviously many other things affect behaviour as well. Culture is the collective set of behaviours in the organization – 'the way we do things around here'.[10]

When we talk about changing culture in a company, we must accept that we are very unlikely to change any individuals' basic beliefs as these get hardwired at a fairly young age. However, we can change quite significantly the ways in which they behave. That's why the definition of organizational culture is the way we **do** things. Over the medium term, we can hire new people whose mindset and beliefs are more consistent with what we are trying to do, or we can encourage those whose mindset and beliefs do not fit with ours to seek employment elsewhere. But that takes time. In the short term, our goal as executives is to work on changing people's day-to-day behaviours and then we can work on changing our processes and incentive systems to try to maintain those behaviours – that's what culture change is all about.

What are the elements of a digital culture or digital mindset? There is no definitive list, but a lot of research has been conducted in this area and there are four qualities that are consistently referenced as follows:

Technology-literate. There are many data scientists in the business world with deep expertise in coding, statistics, analytical methods and AI. And there are many good businesspeople out there with expertise in sales, manufacturing and strategy. But there are remarkably few people who are good in both areas. Looking forward, this has to change. Established companies need to provide digital technology training to all their senior people so that they can ask their data scientists the right questions and interrogate their responses in a productive way. This will allow decision-making to become more data driven.

Open to partnering. This means working with startup companies, research organizations and big-tech companies, and being prepared not to have full control of everything. For example, John described Pearson's journey towards a more open and collaborative approach to innovation in the previous chapter (*see also* page 72).

While partnering with others may sound straightforward, there's a subtle underlying point here. One of the underlying principles of industrial era capitalism was that ownership of assets was vital. Indeed, one influential theory in the academic world is the 'resource based' view of the firm that specifically looks at the quality of a firm's resources and capabilities as the driver of its competitive advantage. But increasingly, in today's business world, the value of the company is a function not so much of the assets that you own as the relationships and partnerships you build. If one looks at the success of ecosystem-based companies like Amazon or Alibaba, they are valuable largely because of the web of relationships they have built with customers, suppliers and third parties. These relationships are what create value.

The point is, it's tricky to shift one's perspective away from 'owning everything' to building value through working with others, yet that is increasingly what's required to succeed in a digital world.

Experimentally minded. This is a point we made in the introduction under the heading 'learn, don't guess' (see also page xxiii). The world is changing quickly, the best way forward is not always clear, so we need to experiment in a rapid way to get to the right result. Another way of making this point is Jeff Bezos' notion of single-door and double-door decisions. A single-door decision is one where once you have gone through it, there is no going back: you are committed to action and if you back out, the cost is substantial. A double-door decision is one where the commitment is low, so you can reverse course with minimal cost. Bezos' point is that most business decisions are double-door decisions and they can and should be delegated to relatively low levels and acted on with relatively little upfront analysis. Top executives should only intervene in single-door decisions. That's part of the philosophy, of course, of trying to be fast-moving; the way it manifests itself is through experimentation.

Comfortable with ambiguity. We quoted F. Scott Fitzgerald earlier, with the notion that the test of a first-rate mind is the ability to hold two opposing ideas at the same time and still be able to function. This is not a mindset that businesspeople are naturally drawn towards – they are much more comfortable working towards a clearly-defined plan and budget – and yet it is increasingly important. When we talk to the recruiters who hire our MBA students, they typically mention tolerance of ambiguity as one of the key traits they are looking for.

Changing Structures and Mindset at Pearson

Let us go full-circle and discuss how these ideas applied in Pearson. Before we started working on this book, John was relatively unfamiliar with the academic research on adhocracy, so it is interesting to consider the ways in which some of these concepts found their way – informally at least – into the day-to-day workings of Pearson.

For example, one of John's key imperatives at Pearson was to encourage people in the idea that 'doing is the best form of thinking'. They asked: how can we get a product into the hands of our customers far faster and earlier? In the spirit of agile, they would get people working in four- to six-week sprints. The team would make their plan, they would test, they would evaluate and then they'd look to go again.

Another point was John's frustration with how major decisions were implemented. For example, even if a decision had been taken to move to a new technology platform or to change our approach to remuneration, many weeks or even months later that decision had either not been implemented, or worse, was being implemented in a half-hearted or intermittent way. Why was this? It's because of what was happening *after the meeting*. Each member of the executive team would subsequently meet with their own teams, who would raise objections about what had been decided. This undermined the confidence of colleagues across the company. It would cause them to reopen and re-debate the issue or to close down debate, uttering the fatal words, '*Well, I agree with you, but it's been decided otherwise, so we'll have to do it.*'

Why are these words fatal? Because there's no real commitment or buy in and at the first sign of trouble, colleagues will want to bail out of whatever it is that's been implemented. During John's tenure, the Pearson executive team agreed on three behaviours that were designed to help make and implement decisions better.

First, they opted for **radical transparency**. They became open much earlier in the context of emerging big decisions, ensuring the wider leadership team and often the whole company understood what the problem or the opportunity was, what was being considered in response and why. It ensured a much higher level of engagement and helped flush out issues and concerns that we may not have considered.

Second, they introduced the concept of **Pearson as the primary family**. It did not matter what role you had when you sat around the executive table, your job was to make the right decision for Pearson overall, not what you thought was best for you or your specific part of the company. You were there as a Pearson leader first and chief technology officer, president of North America, or assistant vice president second.

Third, borrowing from Jeff Bezos, they embraced the idea of '**disagree and commit**'. Each of these three words is equally important. People were encouraged to be much more open and vocal in disagreeing with each other in meetings, especially in the deciding phase. This helped make better decisions quicker because all the issues and perspectives were out there. 'Disagreement', as the author and former CIA analyst Martin Gurri puts it, 'is information – it's a favour you do to me, by calling out the potential gaps and the mistakes in the opinions I hold.'[11]

Once a decision was made, the entire team owned it and they explained to their own teams that all perspectives had been considered, including their own, why this had been decided as the right thing to do for Pearson and how it was everyone's job to now implement it quickly and flawlessly, so it had every chance of being successful. Hence disagree and commit, not disagree but commit. As John recalls:

I tried to model each of these behaviours personally – being as open, honest and communicative as I possibly could be, at every level of the company. I was willing to expose my own doubts and vulnerabilities in the belief that it helped everyone else to do the same and would ultimately make for better decision-making. In my engagements, all levels of the company, I would try to encourage disagreement. If people were critical in a town hall meeting, I would try to welcome and encourage it and address the concerns head-on and hopefully not in a defensive way. I believe that not only was there something to learn, but by being seen to listen to concerns and criticism, I was much more likely to get colleagues to engage, to trust and commit. In meetings with colleagues about subjects relating to their expertise, I would disagree and commit. I would explain why I was concerned about the decision they were making, but having satisfied myself that they'd really thought it through and acknowledging that they knew more about it than I did, I would commit to doing everything I could to make it work.

Crucially, if the path that we had committed to did not work out, I would not under any circumstances say, 'I told you so', but rather would share full responsibility for the outcome and seek to extract learning from it. We should have been explicit about these three behaviours earlier, because by being as transparent and as open as possible, by being explicit about the overriding importance to the primary family and by disagreeing and committing, we made better decisions and implemented them more quickly, leading to better outcomes and thus helping our digital transformation.

CHANGES IN WHERE AND HOW WE WORK: VIRTUAL WORKING

The third aspect of digital work is rethinking where and when we work. During Covid we discovered that it was possible to do almost any work from home and that huge social experiment has arguably changed forever the relationship we have with our workplace.

Plenty of earlier experiments had been done in homeworking. For example, in the late 1990s British Telecom conducted a huge experiment in what they called teleworking; sending hundreds of people to work from home. That experiment did not work, partly for technological reasons, because technology bandwidth was not capable in a way that it is today. However, there were also social reasons why the experiment failed. People who were sent to work from home felt disconnected from those who remained in the office; they felt they were missing out on opportunities.

Large numbers of research studies were done during Covid and it is useful to acknowledge a few of the key findings, from studies that we and others conducted. One key insight is that despite everyone recognizing the challenge of maintaining good personal relationships with colleagues, most managers ended up becoming quite 'blinkered' and task focused. Data from Microsoft, for example, showed that managers became much more siloed during the pandemic than before, focusing more on their existing contacts than new ones and working more asynchronously rather than in real time.[12]

With the pandemic behind us, we are now back in the world of work as we knew before, but with the key difference that a lot of people grew very accustomed to working from home and are therefore reluctant to give it up. Most companies have moved to some form of hybrid working, with people allowed to spend maybe one or two days a week working from home, but we really don't know how this will work out in the medium term, for the companies or the individuals involved. Here are a few pointers for you as you continue to evolve your norms around working from home.

Be clear on why a meeting needs to be in-person. It is intuitively clear that we want people back in the office for relational elements of their work – for example, meetings with customers, mentoring colleagues and for difficult conversations. But it can still be hard to make the case. Many people will ask, why am I coming in for this meeting? Our answer is that in-person meetings are most vital when there is uncertainty about the intended outcome of the meeting and when emotional and non-verbal information is important. In other cases, a Teams or Zoom meeting, or even a call or asynchronous conversation, may be sufficient. The box below explains our thinking.

Invest in relational activities with your remote colleagues. Some people are comfortable working from home at arms-length for weeks on end. We got used to this during Covid and in some areas of work – for example, IT services – such patterns of behaviour are still common. Our advice is not to let them get too distant. Of course, you're checking in with them in terms of the tasks that they're doing. It's important to also continue to have some relational activity with them, which means checking in with them in terms of: how are you feeling? Are you getting the necessary levels of support you need?

Invest in development and growth. During Covid, companies were very good at managing their day-to-day activities, essentially using the people with proven expertise in certain areas and asking them to do more of the same. But for individuals to grow in their organizations, they need a development path. They need an opportunity to sit peripherally in a project team, first of all observing, then getting involved in specific tasks and taking on more responsibility, in an apprentice-like way. That is the process of learning and development that is central to organizational life, but it got lost during Covid. As you think about your hybrid workplace, give special attention to how you give people opportunities to learn and grow and develop. How in particular do you bring new people along, people who have not worked for the company before, some of whom have still not even met face to face, to make sure that they become acculturated to the ways of working in the company?

Explain why showing up is in their best interests. In many companies, senior leaders are encouraging people back to the office, but employees are resisting, having become very comfortable working from home. Some companies have mandated a return to the office. Our preference is to influence and encourage them back by showing that it is in their interests to be present and visible.

Our argument is that high-performing employees engage in what are called extra-role behaviours – things you do on a discretionary basis that are never formalized or written down, for example helping a colleague or taking on an impromptu request. These are the things that get people noticed and indeed get them promoted. And they are extremely hard to engage in when you are working from home.

A couple of years back, the CEO of Morgan Stanley, James Gorman, said, there's a difference between 'job land' and 'career land'. There were people in the company continuing to work remotely in, say, Nebraska rather than New York City. His view was that those people were in job land and would be treated essentially as high-quality contractors. But if people wanted to operate in career land, they needed to be in the office, 'as that is where you're going to have opportunities to connect with people and find opportunities to grow'.[13]

WHEN DO YOU NEED IN-PERSON MEETINGS?

Here is a framework to help you think through when face-to-face interactions are necessary and when doing things virtually works just as well. On the horizontal dimension, there is a measure of the level of complexity of the interaction that you're having with other people. We use the word 'complexity' in a specific way, meaning that there are second- and third-order effects as parts interact in non-linear ways, so it's impossible to predict what the outcomes will be. Some meetings are complex, some are actually very simple and predictable. That is the horizontal dimension from low complexity to high complexity.

The vertical dimension is the extent to which body language and emotion are important. Some interactions are simple and easily codified (for example, sharing information), others are more complex, with body language and emotion conveying huge amounts of information. You put those two dimensions together and you get a sense that certain types of interactions fit in each corner of that matrix.

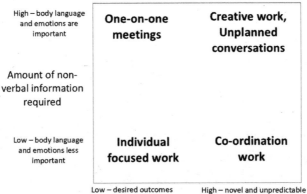

CHARACTERIZING MEETINGS BY THE INTENSITY AND
COMPLEXITY OF THE INTERACTION

High – body language and emotions are important

One-on-one meetings

Creative work, Unplanned conversations

Amount of non-verbal information required

Low – body language and emotions less important

Individual focused work

Co-ordination work

Low – desired outcomes are clear and predictable

High – novel and unpredictable outcomes are desired

Complexity of the interaction required

For example, individual-focused work, such as exchanging emails or writing a blog, is a low emotion interaction with predictable consequences, so it sits in the lower-left corner. In the lower-right corner is co-ordination work – for example, a project planning meeting where we are making sure everybody is following up on what they said they would do. There are interdependencies between tasks, some where there is some complexity, but for the most part it is task-focused and therefore body language and emotion are less important. Many such meetings, even before Covid, were conducted remotely.

An upper-left interaction might be a one-to-one meeting, which might involve giving someone challenging or even negative feedback about their performance. In such cases, you know exactly what you want to do and where you want to end up. However, body language and emotion are incredibly important. You must be able to read that person in a way that helps them to really understand your message – and for them to feel that you are engaging with them as a fellow human being.

An upper-right interaction might be a creative brainstorming session, where people are encouraged to bring their full selves to the meeting, and where the outcome is entirely uncertain. Many of us have tried to participate online in such meetings and they generally don't work well because we cannot read each other's body language properly and the chair or facilitator is reluctant to cede control.

By mapping activities against these two dimensions, you should be in a better position to decide which ones to do in-person and which ones can be done on Zoom or Teams. Clearly, the closer to the upper-right corner, the more important it is to get people together face-to-face.

SUMMARY OF CHAPTER

We noted at the start of this chapter that hierarchical structures emerged in part as a way of channelling information to people as they needed it, so they could do their jobs efficiently. The digital revolution made that function obsolete, thereby opening up the possibility of flatter and more egalitarian workplaces. But hierarchical companies exist for many other reasons as well, many of which are valid but some may be related to the fact that those in positions of power are rarely keen to relinquish it. So, despite all the exciting innovations discussed here, such as agile methods and virtual working, there are still strong forces of inertia keeping things stable. A big part of the leader's job is therefore about bridging the new and the old – embracing some of these innovative ways of working, while keeping the show on the road through established behavioural routines.

It is worth bearing these lessons in mind as we move to the next chapter, which is an in-depth look at the digital technologies that have shaped – and continue to shape – how we work.

5

Investing in Digital Infrastructure: A Non-Technical Guide

This chapter tackles the technical aspects of digital infrastructure but from a non-technical perspective. The challenge many senior executives face is that they simply don't understand digital technology well enough to ask the right questions or to make the right decisions. It is good to trust your chief technology officer or chief information officer, but you also need to hold them to account and to make sure they have understood the business consequences of their IT investment plans. They will also need your support in driving through major changes in the company's technology; you can't provide that support unless you have at least a working understanding of the issues at stake.

Most large incumbent companies have legacy infrastructure problems. It feels like a constant struggle just keeping existing IT systems working, let alone upgrading to new Cloud-based offerings. Meanwhile, your upstart new competitors are running rings round you with mobile-first AI-powered services, all provided at a fraction of the cost of what you are paying.

We start with a cautionary tale from Pearson, the sort of problem that most big incumbents will have experienced at some point as they have gone through an IT transformation programme. We then look at the bigger picture – we look back at the major eras of computer technology and we look forward to what's next, with a discussion of topics like AI and blockchain. Then in the second half of the chapter we provide some advice to incumbent companies in general, and to senior executives in particular, to help them steer a path forward.

PEARSON'S EXPERIENCE

We have already talked about some aspects of Pearson's experience in 're-platforming' the business using state-of-the-art IT infrastructure. At the Big Bets conference in Brooklyn which we discussed earlier in the Introduction, a common refrain of John's fellow CEOs was that their legacy systems meant launching new digital and mobile first products was taking too long and costing too much. They complained that they had so much data, but so little insight – all because their systems were designed for the PC and sometimes even mainframe era, not for the mobile, Cloud-based world in which we now live.

Then in the previous chapter we discussed the huge organizational restructuring Pearson went through, which gives you a sense of the size of the challenge: rationalizing 63 unique enterprise resource planning systems, 93 data centres, 17,000 domains, 120 different ways of creating content etc. It was a huge and disruptive undertaking.

John found out the hard way just how disruptive this restructuring was:

> *It was the spring of 2018 and we were moving our largest enterprise – North American publishing – onto a powerful new system. It would power the fundamentals of how we created, marketed and sold to our customers and how we would then fulfil their orders, invoice them, collect their cash and pay royalties to the authors that we worked with. It was a crucial enabling platform to being a digital first company.*
>
> *It required us to change a complex and fragmented patchwork of legacy systems, some of which were more than 30 years old. This was not an undertaking we took lightly. After a big investment and much planning, we had started 18 months earlier by rolling out the system in smaller markets so we could identify and tackle teething*

problems in ways in which the customer and financial impact of any disruption during implementation were manageable.

We'd involved all stakeholders in many months of planning, we had engaged subject matter experts with specialist knowledge, we had support from a project management consultancy who did nothing but major projects like this. We didn't try to implement across North America all at once – we phased our assessment and virtual school businesses to follow later once we'd bedded in the publishing business and we chose a quieter time in the year to make the change.

We had strict go/no go criteria around go live, with governance that meant three key players – our CFO, CIO and the president of North America publishing – all had to agree.

We went live in early May and initially, everything went well. I was at a board meeting in Milan in mid-June and the head of the external consultancy was giving the go live a rating of 7/10 and urging us to move beyond the intensive support phase of the project and onto business as usual. Our own leaders all seemed to agree. The feedback from the field-based salesforce was reassuring.

It was only two months later that we realized one crucial part of this complex project had gone wrong: we didn't have enough physical stock in the warehouse to fulfil bookstore orders. In implementing the new systems, a crucial interface, linking orders from thousands of bookstores across America into our inventory management team hadn't worked as intended, partly because the bookstores were – understandably from their perspective – reluctant to adapt to a new way of placing orders.

By the time the mistake was identified and rectified, we were in a race against time to meet manufacturing deadlines for the crucial back-to-school window. Now, we wanted to accelerate the shift to digital, but not like this. It was a painful lesson that cost us short term. Some of the students who wanted to buy a new physical book ended up going to the secondary market instead. A few customers were so frustrated that we lost some business for the next academic year. It dented the confidence of colleagues, many of whom had to spend huge amounts of time untangling orders and pacifying angry customers about the lack of physical stock, rather than focusing on the digital future, on how to use the new platform to grow.

This is an example of the risks you face when you change complex long-established legacy systems that are well understood by your own staff and by your customers and partners across the supply chain. And it is why there is such resistance to change. We hated the way we'd let down our customers, our sales teams, our authors and, most of all, our learners. But we were still right to make the change – the long-term benefits still far outweighed the short-term damage caused.

A few weeks later, at the end of a lively town hall meeting at our offices in Hoboken, where we'd had a post-mortem on what had gone wrong, a colleague came up and introduced himself. He explained that he was the software developer maintaining one of the legacy systems which we had just decommissioned. He'd joined Pearson 15 years previously, on a one-year contract, the first time it had been planned to replace the system, which back then was already 25 years old. His contract had been renewed every year since, but he was the only person left who knew how to maintain the system, which was becoming ever harder to do – and it was such old technology nobody wanted to train in it now – and he was ready to retire.

'I know what just happened was painful,' he said, 'but it had to be done. If we hadn't got off UOPs [the legacy system], one day soon it would just have collapsed.'

He was right. There is cost and risk in replacing legacy systems, but there are much bigger costs and risks in not replacing them. Five years on, the company is benefiting hugely from the new systems. New digital products can be launched much faster and cheaper. Data is much more insightful and useful. The re-platforming enabled Pearson to make its own direct to consumer offer, bypassing bookstores and online retailers. And, as an agile, Cloud-based company, where software is essentially a service, it becomes much easier to continuously upgrade platforms rather than face periodic high-risk, sweeping system replacements of the sort we had to do.

BACKGROUND – THE EVOLUTION OF THE COMPUTER
INDUSTRY

Let's provide a little bit of historical context here to help make sense of why upgrading IT systems is such a challenge. For some readers this will be material you know well, for others it should serve as a useful primer.

Using the language of S-curves that we introduced in Chapter 2 (*see also* page 29), the computer industry has gone through three major eras: centralized, decentralized and internet-based:

> *The centralized computing era* in the 1960s and 1970s was dominated by IBM, with a bunch of smaller competitors.[1] It was the era of the mainframe computer – you might have seen pictures of those huge machines in air-conditioned rooms. They were phenomenally expensive, so the priority was to be as efficient with their processing power as possible. Users were allocated time on these machines and they were only used for the most value-added tasks.

> *The decentralized computing era*, also called the personal computing (PC) era, began in the 1980s with the emergence of Apple as the disruptive new brand and Microsoft as the operating system provider behind the PCs of IBM, Dell, Compaq and others. Bill Gates put forward the vision of a computer on every individual's desk and in every office and home. It seemed a crazy idea at the time, because we were used to the centralized model of corporate mainframes. But of course, Gates was right, and through the 1980s and 1990s, there was a proliferation of PCs – the biggest growth industry of its time. This gave all of us access to word processing and spreadsheets at our desks. Companies then built networks of PCs, stringing them together and linking them to their existing mainframe systems. IT companies developed complex and sophisticated ways of getting computers to talk to one another, essentially through a mix of centralized and decentralized activity. This is when the language of 'client server' came into use,

where the client was essentially the machine on your desk and the server was the entity serving you information.

The internet era began in the mid-1990s. While the underlying Internet technology was invented in the 1980s, it was only in 1993, with the invention of the World Wide Web, that companies began to embrace the potential value of the internet. In this period, computers were not just networked together through a corporate IT system, they were connected directly to the information sitting in computers across the world. You might recall the Sun Microsystems slogan at the time, *The Network is the Computer*. Many people were puzzled by this phrase, but it accurately captured the huge shift that was underway.

The internet era made personal computers dramatically more powerful. It allowed you, for example, to get access to information on someone else's computer (Napster, the original music-sharing app, did this, though without thinking through the intellectual property (IP) ownership implications). And of course, it meant you could start to decentralize computing beyond the boundaries of the corporation. We started seeing the emergence of what we nowadays talk about as Cloud computing and software-as-a-service. The big growth stories of the 2000s such as Google, Amazon, and Salesforce succeeded because they figured out ways of providing secure computing services to companies but doing so off-site. They provided the technology 'in the Cloud'. It didn't really matter where the Cloud was (indeed, some companies have their Cloud services on their own premises). The point is, computing services began to resemble other utilities like water and electricity, available at the flick of a switch, without any worries about software upgrades and fixing bugs.

Of course, this is a vastly simplified account, but it illustrates the profound shifts in IT infrastructure that have occurred during our lifetimes. And the real challenge is that today we are still dealing – to some degree – with all three simultaneously. Large companies like Pearson, who have been around for more than 50 years or so, have hardware and software from each era. There are still big banks out there running core operations on ancient coding languages developed in the 1960s, such as COBOL and FORTRAN, because the costs and complexities involved in changing them are so daunting.

WHAT'S NEXT IN THE DIGITAL WORLD?

This brief historical account begs an obvious question – what's next? Clearly internet computing with Cloud-based infrastructure isn't the last step in the evolution of digital technology. There are huge amounts of investment going into new technologies all the time and as a senior executive you want to be up to date on all these new developments, even if they are too embryonic for you to invest in them yet.

We are cautious about saying too much here, partly because our expertise is at the applied end of the spectrum, not on the underlying technologies, and partly because things change so rapidly in this space. But it is useful to speculate a bit on what the next era of computing might look like. Here are four of the candidates. For each one we offer a layperson's description of what it is, reasons to be excited, reasons to be sceptical and a final prognosis.

Blockchain. This is often described as a distributed ledger – in other words, it's a store of information (a ledger) that is replicated exactly on multiple computers around the world (distributed). Users can access this information, but they cannot tamper with it. And this gives it important advantages, at least in some circumstances, as a single immutable source of truth.

The first well-known use of this technology was to create cryptocurrencies such as bitcoin, with the blockchain essentially being an immutable record of all financial transactions between parties using a cryptocurrency. Many other use-cases have also been developed: for example, keeping track of individual identities, the sources of valuable products such as diamonds and international currency transfers.

Reasons to be excited. The genius of blockchain technology is not the storing of value or information in digital form (there were digital currencies before blockchain). Rather, it is the creation of a mechanism for storing information in immutable form *without a central entity having control over it.* Before blockchain, there was always some sort of central authority who had privileged access to the ledger in question and users ultimately had to trust that the authority would act in everyone's best interests. For example, we must trust our bank to store our money and we must trust the government to keep our identity secure. However, this puts enormous power into the hands of central authorities, a situation that many people find objectionable. What if companies used their monopolistic power to make excessive profit and drive out competition? What if governments encroached on the rights and freedoms of citizens? Blockchain technology is potentially the antidote to all these concerns. It is a way of taking control (of money, information and other resources) away from a few powerful institutions and sharing it with thousands of individuals across society.

Reasons to be sceptical. Blockchain has not lived up to its hype, for several reasons. The underlying technology for maintaining a distributed ledger is expensive and slow. Without getting into the technicalities, the current way of ensuring that no central entity takes control of a distributed ledger (called 'proof of work') is too energy-intensive to scale up and it cannot handle the large volumes of transactions undertaken by centrally controlled systems. Governments and central banks are very worried about shadow currencies emerging as they would lose control of money supply and interest rates and would be unable to stop money laundering and fraud. There have also been some spectacular blow-ups in the cryptocurrency world, with the collapse in 2022 of FTX, the third largest cryptocurrency exchange in the world, being the most recent example.

Prognosis. Blockchain is here to stay. Many companies have fully functioning blockchain systems for certain activities. For example, J.P. Morgan has an information exchange network called Liink and

Rio Tinto has a platform called Start for keeping track of materials along a value chain. But a key point is that these are 'permissioned' blockchains, meaning there is a central entity overseeing the use of them. This means that some of the benefits of a blockchain, such as transparent and immutable records, are being realized, but others, notably the freedom from central control, are not.

It seems highly likely that bitcoin and other cryptocurrencies will continue to exist on the fringes of the world's financial system. If new attempts to regulate the crypto industry in the US succeed, it could even start to gain greater traction. Companies and banks will continue to refine the blockchain technology and gradually sensible use-cases will emerge. But the threat of blockchain shaking up entire industries has receded. In the language used earlier in the book, blockchain is turning out to be a sustaining not a disruptive technology.

Metaverse. This is a *virtual* shared space for people to interact in. Online multi-player games like World of Warcraft or League of Legends are the best-known metaverse applications. Many people will also recall Second Life, which was launched earlier in the internet era as a place where people might conduct business, take lectures, or go on dates, all through their personal avatar.

The concept of the metaverse goes back to the early 1990s, but the term was popularized by Mark Zuckerberg in 2021 when Facebook was renamed Meta Platforms and he spent a fortune promoting the notion that an increasing amount of our time would be spent in the metaverse.

Reasons to be excited. Several of the big trends in society point towards us spending increasing amounts of our time in the metaverse. Internet access is becoming ubiquitous; virtual reality and augmented reality technology are rapidly improving; many people live in cramped cities with limited personal space and are looking for escapist opportunities. The 2018 sci-fi movie *Ready Player One* painted a compelling picture of the attractions of the metaverse. The big technology companies are also propelling us down this path; aside from Zuckerberg, Apple recently launched the Vision Pro headset and Amazon has created an Amazon Anywhere virtual retail experience. There are also big industrial applications in the metaverse – for example, digital twins of factories and the use of augmented reality for training and supporting technicians.

Reasons to be sceptical. For all the hype, the metaverse simply hasn't taken off. Estimates suggest Facebook/Meta has spent $36 billion on building its metaverse, with little to show for it.[2] While a segment of the population continues to enjoy the escapism of online gaming, the rest of us are ambivalent about screen time and headsets. The rapid bounce-back in travel, eating out and live events post-Covid is testament to our basic need for real-world social interaction.

Prognosis. There will continue to be improvements in virtual and augmented reality technologies, and practical applications of these technologies will proliferate in both the consumer-facing and industrial parts of the economy. But Zuckerberg's metaverse vision will not play out in the way he was anticipating. The term metaverse has already lost much of its lustre.

Web3. This is the third generation of the World Wide Web (the system which allows documents to be shared and connected over the internet). The first generation (Web1) involved people and companies broadcasting information and engaging in transactions and was typified by e-commerce sites like Amazon and eBay. The second generation (Web2) involved large amounts of user-generated content and interactivity and was typified by social network sites like Facebook and TikTok. Web3 is a user-centric version of what we have now, which gives every individual control over their data and interactions. It relies to a large degree on blockchain technology to manage all this personal data.

Reasons to be excited. Many people are worried about the excessive control that Google, Facebook, Microsoft and Amazon have over our information and our lives (and in China, there are similar concerns about Tencent, Byte Dance and Alibaba). Web3 is the antidote to this overweening power: 'In theory a blockchain-based web could shatter the monopolies on who controls information, who makes money, and even how networks and corporations work.'[3] As with all things digital, there are hundreds of startups working on the decentralized architecture that will make Web3 possible.

Reasons to be sceptical. Web3 relies on blockchain technology to take off, so the concerns about scalability noted above also apply here. There is also a fundamental behavioural problem with Web3, namely that a lot of people like the convenience of the integrated Web experience provided by Microsoft, Google or WeChat. If you want to control all your personal information and interact with other Web users outside of the orbit of a tech giant, you can do so but you need technical knowledge and it takes more time. Many startup companies have emerged in the Web3 space, but none has really taken off yet as they lack the user-friendliness to reach beyond the geek community.

Prognosis. While we may have worries about the dominance of the tech giants, most of us are comfortable with the Faustian bargain we have struck (they get access to our information, we get an easy-to-use digital interface). So even if the technical challenges with Web3 are resolved, we can expect the likes of Google and Microsoft to maintain their influence over our lives by offering, for example, services with greater individual data protection. In short, Web3 won't take off in the way its proponents are arguing. Of course, the Web will continue to evolve, but in directions that are currently unforeseeable.

Artificial intelligence. AI is the simulation of human capabilities by machines and it has been part of the technology landscape since the 1960s. In the early days of the computer revolution, we marvelled at how quickly computers could do difficult arithmetic calculations, then we were excited by their voice simulation and logical reasoning capabilities. In recent years, computers have achieved human-like levels of voice and image recognition. Now, thanks to the arrival of ChatGPT in November 2022, we are understandably impressed with the quality of text, image creation and coding that it can produce.

The point is that our image of what AI is keeps shifting. Someone once defined AI as 'what computers cannot do yet' because once it's part of the computer's functionality, the mystique is gone. This helps to put ChatGPT into perspective. Its capabilities are amazing, but it is just the latest chapter in a very long book and we can be sure our children's generation won't be as impressed as we are that a computer can write fluent text responses to our questions.

It goes without saying that AI technology is improving all the time but progress is somewhat unpredictable. Historically, AI has gone through periods where little happened ('AI winter') and then periods of rapid improvement ('AI spring'). It is also unclear in advance what types of human skills AI will be able to replicate. It turns out that many of the things humans find easy are hard for AI to do, and vice versa (this is called Moravec's paradox).[4] All of which makes it hard for business executives to decide where and when to make investments in AI.

Reasons to be excited. As we discuss later on in Chapter 7, the explosion of interest in ChatGPT in early 2023 was like nothing we have seen since the invention of the World Wide Web in 1993. And even before ChatGPT, there was huge excitement of the potential to apply AI in such areas as image recognition, fraud prevention, simultaneous translation and document processing. Without getting into the technicalities, we have seen breakthroughs in machine learning (how computers process and interpret data), coupled with exponential increases in processing power and in the amount of data available (which computers are trained on). These trends compound on one another, so we can anticipate dramatic improvements in the months and years ahead. Some observers predict singularity (when AI reaches the same level as human intelligence) within 20 years.[5]

Reasons to be sceptical. The field of AI has always been a fertile ground for speculation and imagination. We are all familiar with the science fiction writers who have sketched out utopian and dystopian views of a future where humans and machines coexist. Scenarios that previously seemed far-fetched or futuristic must now be taken seriously. Things that we have always considered uniquely human – language, reason, art – can now be mimicked by AI in ways that could undermine our shared culture and institutions and threaten societal cohesion. These fears are leading to a big global debate as to how generative AI should be regulated, with governments around the world acting unusually quickly to develop guardrails around the use of AI in business and social settings. Many companies are already developing policies committing them to the 'responsible' and 'ethical' use of AI. This debate is made even more complicated by the speed of development and adoption of AI. Although, as a business leader, you should be aware of the wider political and regulatory context, your most important task is to focus on what AI can do for you today and over the next couple of years. And the reality is that today's state-of-the-art is Narrow AI, which does one specific thing well, such as creating text or computer coding, or controlling an autonomous vehicle. General AI that is human-like in its capacity to do different things is still some way off.

Prognosis. Compared to blockchain, metaverse and Web3, the potential impact of AI on the business world is very high. Every business executive today needs to be experimenting with tools like ChatGPT themselves and to be thinking about how and when to invest in these technologies. We discuss some of the short and medium implications of generative AI later on in Chapter 7.

To summarize. We have talked about four big technology areas that have captured a lot of interest in recent years and there are several others we chose not to address as they have narrower or more technical characteristics (for example, Internet of Things, 3D print-ing, quantum computing). And in many cases, we find ourselves sitting on the more sceptical side of the table – we understand the arguments that proponents of these new technologies are making, but with the likely exception of artificial intelligence, they will mostly fail to live up to their hype.

IMPLICATIONS FOR COMPANIES

We have done a brief retrospective on the evolution of computer technology and provided a glimpse of the future. This provides useful context and some insights into where you might place your bets in the years ahead, but let us now return to the present day and the challenges you face as an incumbent company. Like Pearson, at the beginning of this chapter, you are trying to stay on top of the ever-evolving infrastructure landscape. The costs of maintaining your legacy systems are huge. Bank executives we talk to reckon they spend up to 30 per cent of their IT budget simply keeping their old systems running, papering over the cracks and fixing bugs. There is also, in most cases, a patchwork of systems that have been stitched together over the years and don't talk to each other properly. You also have a nagging worry that the systems you are running aren't aligned around the actual needs of your users. Everything just about works, but in a clunky, sub-optimized fashion whereas your new competitors, who built their systems from scratch five years ago, are more user-focused, agile and efficient at the same time.

So, what's your IT infrastructure strategy? Clearly there are entire books written on this single question, so we won't be able to do full justice to it here. But from our discussions with CIOs and CTOs, and our experience, we can highlight some important general points.

Sort your data out first

It is tempting to reach for the big levers of change straight away – for example, shifting your IT systems onto the Cloud or investing in the latest AI technology. But for most established companies, the necessary first step is to tidy up and quality assure your existing data. Data governance is the term usually used here and the evidence suggests most companies have a lot of room for improvement. One McKinsey study estimated employees spent around 30 per cent of their time on non-value-added tasks due to poor data quality and availability.[6]

Julian recalls working with one client, a large automotive company that had bought an AI platform from Palantir, a US analytics company. They were looking for opportunities to use this platform in efficiency and quality improvement projects across the company, but the managers charged with doing the work quickly became frustrated because the necessary data was fragmented and had not been cleaned up for years. There was a two-year delay to the work while the data problems were resolved.

The executives we interviewed for this book all talked about data. Danny Attias, CTO at London Business School, said:

Fundamentally, anyone who's involved in digital technology must be focusing on high-quality clean data, that's the prerequisite. Until you have your data sorted, it's garbage in, garbage out.

Albert Hitchcock, former CIO at Pearson, concurred:

If you don't have good data, then you are trying to personalize based on poor information and you're not going to deliver a great experience. Cleaning up data is one of the biggest challenges for established organizations.

Unfortunately, there is no shortcut solution to cleaning up messy data. It is painstaking, labour-intensive work and in large companies, it can take years. It's also worth noting that responsibility for having clean data doesn't just lie with the IT department. Danny Attias again:

Do you have the people to provide you with high-quality data? I don't mean three data scientists sitting in a room. I mean 10 per cent, 20 per cent, 30 per cent of your workforce who understand how to handle data and how to get it more efficient. And do you have a culture within your organization that encourages people to understand what questions you want to answer? Then as you start to become more mature on that, you can start to think about automation, predictive modelling and such like. But that's at the very end of the maturity curve and most organizations are still at the lower end.

Embrace Cloud services

One of the biggest areas of growth in IT spend over the last 20 years has been Cloud computing services, pioneered by Amazon Web Services, with Google Cloud, Microsoft Azure and others following rapidly. It is now standard practice across most sectors of the economy to buy 'infrastructure as a service' from one of these giants, so that your entire stack of software services is then provided to you from a metaphorical cloud, in a similar way to sourcing your gas and electricity from the local power utility.

Consider the example of Enel, the Italian energy company we discussed much earlier in the book, and specifically, the transformation programme brought about by Carlo Bozzoli, who was hired as CIO in 2015. As he explained:

ICT (information and communication technology) at Enel had traditionally been seen as an internal service provider to users who had almost no choice but to bring to the department requests to fix, augment or replace products in use. The ICT team's workload tended to consist of evaluating issues, resetting passwords and generally being the gatekeeper to the business; a systems administrator in name and function.

Carlo resolved to transform how IT services were provided, so that Enel could become more customer-focused and streamlined. Having established the basics of data governance were in place, his first move was a migration of all of Enel's applications to the Cloud. He started in Italy, announcing his plans at an all-hands meeting of the 70 Italy-based ICT managers less than 24 hours after assuming his new role. He outlined his vision, then faced an hour and a half of questions from managers worried about the impact of the change.

Carlo tasked a cross-functional team with creating a list of every application across Enel and how it interacted within the ecosystem. He involved Enel's external service providers in this process, as they had around 400 people working on the applications through business process outsourcing (BPO) contracts – he wanted to begin the move before the contracts with these providers expired.

Next, a team evaluated Cloud service providers. Settling on Amazon Web Services, they began shutting down the Italian data centres, migrating applications to the Cloud and retraining employees. In parallel, Bozzoli and his team engaged with the trade unions to show them how employees could be productively reassigned after they were trained. As a result of this process, Enel was able to reduce the number of applications used from 1,850 to 1,200. This rationalization process allowed Enel to leave BPOs without any change in the number of Enel ICT employees. Significant financial savings also followed.

So, what are the benefits of putting your systems on the Cloud? The first is ease of use, which is particularly attractive to smaller companies. As Albert Hitchcock said,

> *It's been an amazing transformation, the adoption of Cloud. The reason it's been so successful is just because of the ease with which you can adopt these technologies. In the past, we had to build everything ourselves. Now you can pay your credit card online and have virtual machines up and running within minutes. Quite an incredible change.*

A second and related point is the capacity to adapt your IT expenditure according to demand. Albert Hitchcock again:

> *One of the things the Cloud has done is it has democratized the availability of computing resources so you can scale up and scale down in a more cost-effective way. It comes down to how you design your products and services, but if you use auto-scaling, you're only buying the computer capacity as you need it.*

Third, there is the reassurance that you are staying on top of the latest technological developments because your vendor is at the forefront. Danny Attias, CTO at London Business School:

> *The fact is that organizations like Microsoft are spending tens of billions of dollars per year on cybersecurity and AI. If you invest yourself into their stack or the Amazon stock or a Google stack and you implement the best standards and you use the right technologies, then you can rely on them to a degree to take care of a lot of things for you.*

Of course, Cloud computing brings plenty of challenges as well. One is a shift in mindset and capability, with people needing different skills to work through a partner rather than do everything themselves.

There is the concern that you are overly reliant on one big company like AWS or Microsoft. Some companies in fact use more than one Cloud provider to avoid overdependency on one vendor. Also, the cost isn't necessarily lower – Cloud services can be very expensive if you have spiky and unpredictable demand, so it is critical to be clear in advance what workload you anticipate from your provider.

Develop a user perspective

In Chapter 3 we talked briefly about the importance of design thinking (*see also* page 73). Many products and services are developed from an inside-out perspective based on what we think the world needs. Design thinking takes an outside-in perspective, starting with the often unarticulated needs of the user.

The IT industry has a slightly different formulation of the same idea. It is called Conway's law, named after Melvin Conway, an American computer scientist in the 1960s.[7] He said that 'organizations, who design systems are constrained to produce designs which are copies of the communication structures of these organizations.' For example, centralized organizations tend to create centralized IT systems. But it's the corollary that's important, namely once you have a centralized IT system, you end up operating in a top-down way, even if the marketplace has started demanding a more decentralized service.

When working on an IT transformation, then, you need to revisit the strategic priorities in the company to make sure your transformation efforts are working to support those priorities rather than cutting across them. And often that means a significant change in how IT is organized.

Consider the next stage in Enel's transformation under Carlo Bozzoli. Once the Cloud migration was underway, he moved on to the second phase of work; namely the creation of 13 digital hubs – teams of IT specialists – working directly with their respective business units. The idea was that, by decentralizing these teams, their responsiveness to business needs would increase dramatically. The digital hubs would report to both their business unit and to Carlo. He explained how this new structure was aligned to Enel's broader goals:

Our digital strategy was built on three objectives: creating intelligent generation and distribution infrastructure (assets), developing a new 'smart' offering while deploying a next-generation experience (customers) and adopting the new customer-centric paradigm to Enel employees (people). To do this we focused on three enablers – IT platforms built on a global company standard, Cloud infrastructure to help us scale up and down, and cybersecurity.

While it could have seemed to outsiders that the ICT organization was being dismantled, in fact we ICT-ized the entire company.

This user-centred approach makes good sense, but it's not easy to do because it requires a great deal of planning and preparatory work before you are ready to implement any changes and it also means stopping people from making their own ad hoc changes. As Danny Attias commented:

Once you have a lot of people with no governance starting to automate things left, right and centre, then you just create spaghetti and dependencies, which ultimately become a noose around your neck. There is an old idea that we use technology to automate processes to generate an immediate efficiency saving. But actually, what we should be doing is re-engineering those processes altogether and figuring out what is the problem we're trying to solve.

A final point on this user-centred perspective is that it's much easier to put in place when your infrastructure is well-designed in a modular way. Modularity means having many self-contained elements that can be combined with minimal effort, because the interfaces between modules have been carefully thought through.

Enel again provides a good example. Through Carlo Bozzoli's restructuring, the number of different systems had been reduced by 75 per cent, leaving a relatively small number of key platforms (a few dozen) all operating 100 per cent on Cloud infrastructure. This made it possible to create combinations of systems that could be deployed rapidly in any market through a 'plug-and-play' model.

For example, one global platform managed Enel's energy distribution business across geographies, while another was used to manage customer interactions in all markets. These platforms were also used for emerging business opportunities, such as e-Mobility. As Carlo explained,

> *Our platformization strategy isn't just about doing things more efficiently today – it enables us to move much more quickly in the future as new business models start to emerge.*

Finally, the notion of experimentation which has been a theme throughout the book also applies here. Annette Thomas, former managing director of the Guardian Media Group, shared her reflections on new technology deployment:

> *Rather than rushing ahead and being aggressive, we really tried to focus on what would be a great experiment to understand how this works. How can we understand how to deploy this technology in a meaningful way for our customers or for our employees and how could we test this in short, fast experiments without being overly seduced by its potential?*

Get the best out of your people

Another theme from earlier chapters is that digital transformation is as much about people as it is about technology. We talked about agile working in Chapter 4, for example, as an example of a novel and progressive way of working and it's important not to forget that the concept originated in IT world. To be specific, the agile manifesto (www.agilemanifesto.org) was put together by a progressive group of software coders in 1999 and included statements such as 'we have come to value individuals and interactions over processes and tools'.

Enormous progress has been made over the intervening years in applying and refining the principles of agile software development. The evidence suggests there are genuine and lasting benefits from agile, in terms of both efficiency and effectiveness. There are also motivational benefits, with most people preferring a style of working that gives them greater autonomy and control over their own agenda.

The people we interviewed in writing this book largely concurred with this general view. Enel, for example, used agile methods in large parts of its ICT function, though mostly in a hybrid form that included a moderate level of top-down steering. In terms of outcomes, speed to market improved from mid-2018 to mid-2019, with lead times of 'epics' (agile projects) and user stories decreasing from five weeks to 0.75 weeks during that year.

Albert Hitchcock at Pearson offered a nuanced view of agile. In terms of the reason to use it, it was the cross-functional collaboration that he felt was most important:

> What we're really trying to do is get the person who's thinking about the experience, the software developer, someone from cybersecurity, the operational person; we want to get them all in the same team, thinking about the solution and actually building the capability hand in glove.

He also felt that the push for entirely self-managed teams was a bit extreme:

> My view is there's still a role for good project management in agile. A lot of people say, ditch waterfall, move to agile. In reality, you still need to keep a track on progress. You still need to understand how you're delivering milestones for customers; you still need to keep an eye on cost. There is still a project management responsibility, particularly in large programmes, but you want to decouple them from the people who are thinking about experience and software development, and how to bring these things to life.

Our view is simply there is no best way and we are extremely wary of consultants who take a dogmatic approach to how agile must be done. Every organization has its own distinctive history and culture, and what works in one will not necessarily work in the other. What matters is understanding the key principles – for example, the importance of cross-functional teams and the power of allowing teams to define their own short-term priorities, and then adapting those principles to the demands of the situation.

MANAGING THE DIGITAL AGENDA IN THE BOARDROOM

The final part of this chapter focuses specifically on the role of the non-technical executive at the top who is seeking to make good judgements on the company's IT investments.

Julian's experience as a member of the senior management team at London Business School 15 years ago is instructive. On every other aspect of running the school – from programmes to HR, from finance to estates – he could drill down and understand every detail of what was going on. But when the CIO was in the boardroom talking about the School's IT systems, the executive team's eyes started to glaze over because the situation was complicated, their knowledge base was limited and the CIO wasn't great at explaining things. The senior team didn't know how to ask the really probing questions about the detail of the technology choices he was advocating.

LBS's senior executives weren't alone in their ignorance and confusion. There are many industries where senior people are experts in almost all the different aspects of their work, but the IT function remains a 'black box' to them. It's therefore important to be thoughtful about getting the right competence around the table so that we can make smart judgements and careful trade-offs about the management of all our digital infrastructure.

So, what's our advice? First, you need to be clear with your chief information officer (CIO) what you expect from them. Some companies are still looking for a CIO just to 'sort out the technology'. That can be a workable arrangement if your IT is already in good shape, or if your industry is relatively low-tech. But increasingly, this approach is likely to be a bit short-sighted because as we have said most industries have huge demands for more and more thoughtful IT investment so it's usually smart to find a CIO who can become a strategic partner to the CEO and the other executives. Here is how Danny Attias talks about it:

> *The role of the CIO in that boardroom is to help influence the culture so that they see what's really needed. In the boardroom we talk a lot about prioritization, it's our job to define the priorities. Often in a legacy culture, I'll say we don't have the luxury of talking about priorities because it's dependencies that are holding us back. We want to do this, but we can't do this until we do that. So, it's about accepting where we're at, what needs to be done and then going on that journey.*

Second, it's useful to think about the optics of who sits around the boardroom table and what jobs they have. Some companies don't have a CIO on the executive board – it's common for them to report to the CFO, for example. But assuming you want digital technology sitting around the top table – and if you are planning a digital transformation, you should – you have an array of options for what you call the role: CIO (information), CTO (technology), CDO (digital), CAIO (artificial intelligence), CISO (information security) are all well-established acronyms and there are probably others as well. The choice is as much about signalling as anything, i.e. telling people internally and externally what your priorities are. But it's also worth noting there are two different flavours of role here. CIOs typically have a big budget and are accountable for delivering IT projects on schedule. CDOs, by contrast, usually find themselves in cross-cutting staff roles, with a big strategic agenda to make the company more digital, but very little authority over others. Many of the CDOs we have met in multi-billion-dollar companies have only 10–20 people reporting to them.

Another tactic is to get input from multiple sources, especially in the emerging areas of technology. One technique John used at Pearson was the creation of a digital advisory network, as mentioned in the previous chapter (*see also* page 73). This was a group of external people that came from Big Tech companies, venture capital,

131

startup companies and academia, who had been involved in a lot of digital innovation and could look at the challenges from a whole range of different perspectives – for example, what digital meant for customers, or how you frame the digital narrative for shareholders. The network was co-chaired by John, as CEO and a non-executive board director who himself had a digital background.

SUMMARY OF CHAPTER

Let's close this chapter with some overarching lessons based on all the above.

Fix the roof when the sun is shining. Re-platforming should be a continuous, ongoing process. Upgrading digital infrastructure is not something a company should do once a decade. You should be doing it all the time – and the more you can do when the business is going well and there isn't a compelling pressure to invest, the better. You want to have the digital infrastructure in place ahead of changes in product or business model. You really don't want to have to be doing everything all at the same time.

Digital transformation, not digitization. Gavin Patterson, whom we quoted earlier, makes this point very well. Do not simply digitize your existing processes and ways of working. Use the digital software to simplify and streamline processes and to eliminate redundant actions. Take a fresh look at the data you're collecting – less is often more and certainly much easier to analyse and act on. So, ask yourself: do we really need all the data we're collecting? Walk through the process from a customer perspective – are we applying digital to make it a simple, easy and pleasurable user experience?

Simplify and standardize as much as you possibly can. Everybody thinks their business is special and different. Sometimes they're right, most often they're wrong. Innovation, creativity and diversity should be completely focused on product and service differentiation that will be valued by the customer, not on the underlying platforms that support the business.

Simplification and standardization enable you to scale the very best digital infrastructure. It frees up resources to invest where it will have the biggest difference and makes it much easier to integrate acquired businesses. And when you acquire a new business, bring it on to the company infrastructure as quickly as possible and with little, if any, customization.

Resource and train properly. Digital transformation means that investing in infrastructure needs to be matched by investing in your people – backfilling roles so that subject matter experts can really engage in simplifying and streamlining processes, training people properly on how to use the new systems, recognizing that major system changes bring stress and risk, and providing plenty of time and support. Skimping on any of this is asking for trouble. If you're investing in powerful new digital tools, you must ensure your people are able to use them. You must invest in them, too.

Leadership needs to be fully aligned. The CEO, CFO, CIO and the commercial leaders of the business all need to be fully and actively engaged at every stage of the process – and especially in times of stress and when things go wrong. New digital infrastructure should not be something that IT *does* to a business, so it feels it is being imposed on it. It must be done in partnership with it. The devil is in the detail, so it is important that everyone is really listening and learning from each other – and that we all fully understand the consequences of the changes that we are making.

As we have said many times already, digital transformation is about much more than just technology, but you need to understand enough about the technology to make good strategic and organizational decisions. That was the purpose of this chapter. In the next chapter we shift our focus towards the overall leadership agenda.

6

Leading Change: The People and Cultural Challenge

Many writers have observed that leadership is a lonely job. You can take a lot of advice and feedback along the way, but at critical points you have to make decisions that not everyone will agree with and you must take responsibility for the consequences.

Throughout this book, we have sought to emphasize the behavioural and political dimensions of digital transformation – that it's not just about the technology. In this chapter we focus on the leader's role in steering change and we offer advice on the tactics needed to stay on top of process. Much of this advice comes from John's eight years as CEO of Pearson, involving a gut-wrenching transformation and making it very hard to keep employees and external stakeholders on board with the changes that needed to be made. We also bring in concepts from academic literature and examples from other top executives to help you build up a holistic picture of the leadership challenge.

ARE WE THERE YET?

Let's start with John's reflections on of the big challenges he faced in leading Pearson's transformation.

As Pearson's digital transformation gathered pace, more and more time was spent meeting colleagues around the world to explain what we were doing and why, to listen to their ideas, to answer their questions and to recognize and try to address their concerns. The size of the meetings would vary. Virtual town hall meetings were attended by over 5,000 colleagues in countries all over the world while physical town hall meetings, at each of our major locations had hundreds of people attending, right down to intimate gatherings of just a few individuals.

The specifics of what was discussed would change too, depending on the location and the types of colleagues involved. What never changed was that someone would always ask a variation on the same question. Are we there yet? Are we finished changing yet? When will we know that the transformation is now complete? When can we get back to living our regular working lives?

If you think about it, it's a perfectly rational question to ask. In Pearson's 175-year history, the company had evolved tremendously. The company would go through episodic periods of change, from buying or selling a company, entering or exiting a country or market, adapting a new technology, adjusting to major changes in the economy or the wider world. Each event would be destabilizing for a while, then everything would settle down again for an extended period that would feel static and stable.

However, if it was an obvious question to ask, it was a difficult one to answer. For the truth was, we were not just changing one thing at a time about the company, we were changing pretty much everything at the same time – our products and how we created them, what we charged for them, how we sold and marketed them, how we thought about our customers and how we engaged with them, how we were organized and all the systems and processes that supported our businesses. We were doing this in response to the huge changes that were happening in our industry and the wider world. None of these changes had an obvious endpoint. It felt like we would have to continue changing at an ever-faster rate for as long into the future as we could see.

It was only upon reading Tom Friedman's book, Thank You For Being Late, that we could put what we were living through in a wider context.[1] Friedman attributes to John Kelly, a senior IBM executive, the idea that while humans are used to living in a linear world *where things change in a steady and predictable way, technology is exponential, accelerating at a pace that can be exhilarating, at least for a short while, but soon leaves us feeling uncertain and uncomfortable. Closing the gap between that exponential digital change and the linear pace of human adaptation is a major leadership challenge.*

We were all feeling under extreme pressure, everybody was so busy, everything was happening so fast, it felt overwhelming. At the start of my tenure as CEO, I'm not sure I could have spelt correctly the word 'discombobulated' or easily have pronounced it. By the end of it, the word tripped readily off my tongue as it captured very well the confused, uncertain and disoriented state that the latest changes had often tipped one or other part of the company into. We weren't the only people feeling this way. At the Big Bets gathering in Brooklyn [see also the introductory chapter, page xii], *my fellow CEOs would bemoan the fact that while they were investing billions in digital platforms, they felt they still had the same analogue culture and organization using them. Many complained they had been bruised from head to toe, trying to change their internal culture.*

There are three features of change that make it so challenging. First, change itself is messy and uncertain. Implementing something well is extremely difficult. The changes you are making to accelerate digital transformation are often at precisely the same time or just ahead of the analogue business experiencing the market pressures that necessitate the change. Internally and externally, people confuse correlation – we're having to accelerate digital change because the analogue business is under pressure – with causation: that it's the changes that we're making which are causing the problem rather than being a vital part of the long-term solution. And so, people can lose faith.

Second, none of the changes you make happen in a vacuum. In today's interconnected world more than ever, no company – no person – is an island. We are all, in the words of the poet John Donne, 'a piece of the continent, a part of the main'. The customers you serve and the markets you operate in are also in a state of flux and are responding to the same changes that you are grappling with.

It often means that changes you make may need to be accelerated or even sometimes reversed mid-flight. For example, we created a new global product organization to help co-ordinate and drive the overall analogue-to-digital transition. Within a few years, however, it became clear that the analogue business was under severe financial pressure more quickly than anticipated and this meant that we could not afford the cost of running a large global product organization. In any event, with the major changes to the global technology stack and platforms now made, it made much more sense to have a smaller, more agile global product team and embed more of the digital development within each major sales lead product line. This is a great example of the maxim that if the facts change, the right thing to do is to change your mind. Understandably, colleagues can find such constant change and churn disconcerting.

The third point is that colleagues are desperate for the process to be finite because they find the constant changes so exhausting and just too much to cope with; hence the notion of 'Change Fatigue'. There was a reason why in that final email to all peers and colleagues, I quoted Bob Dylan, 'He or she, not busy being born is busy dying' and wrote that 'Pearson has been busy, being born for 175 years, and long may that continue.' I knew that my successor would want – and would need – to change some of the decisions I had made and I wanted to make it easier for colleagues to embrace rather than resist those changes.

It is not unusual for senior leaders going through a major digital transformation to be somewhat dismissive of middle management in the company, who they often perceive as getting in the way of, or even thwarting, radical change. The argument you'll often hear is that senior management has a clear vision of the digital future and the rank and file of the organization – many of whom, at an earlier stage in their career and thus more likely to be digital natives – 'get it'. The problem of inertia, the argument goes, sits with layers of middle managers who act as 'a permafrost', protecting their own positions and established ways of working, undermining the grand vision and slowing down the urgent need for change, preventing it from being translated into day-to-day action. Early in my tenure, I may even have been inclined to share this perception. With time, I realized it was absolutely the wrong way to think about it.

In all the employee 'pulse' surveys we did to gauge the mood of the organization, it was middle management that was consistently the highest regarded for their leadership. They were the 'shock absorbers' of the company – the people that had to both translate grand visions and strategies into practical, pragmatic reality, while reassuring and empathizing with their teams, who were often bewildered and confused by the scale of the changes internally and the market turmoil externally. The longer I served as CEO, the more time I spent with middle management, listening and learning from them and taking the time to explain what we were doing and why. Their role is crucial in any digital transformation.

WHY IS TRANSFORMATION BECOMING HARDER?

Let's step back from the Pearson story and reflect on the challenge of transformation in a specifically digital context. We offer three points of context.

First, the rate of technological change is increasing. We have all heard the statement that 'change is happening more quickly than it used to' and there is some reason to think this may just be hyperbole. However, there is also some evidence to support it. For example, if we look at companies influenced by digital technology, all these changes are underpinned by Moore's Law.[2] (This is the fact that the number of transistors on a chip essentially doubles every 18 months and this has been going on now for 40 years.)

The speed with which various technologies *diffuse* across the population is also speeding up. One fascinating study looked at the speed with which households in the US gained access to various consumer products. For televisions, it took some 60 years for 50 per cent of the US population to have a television set. For personal computers, it took 19 years, for internet technology 10 years, and so on.[3] ChatGPT then broke all records, with the first million users reached in just five days. This increasing speed is not an illusion – any company working in the digital technology space must accept that there are accelerating cycles of diffusion of new technology.

Second, people are uncomfortable with rapid change. It creates anxiety as discussed above and also creates a knowledge gap as the available stock of information on any given topic grows far more quickly than any individual's capacity to assimilate it. That knowledge gap must be filled, not just by each of us individually learning, but by harnessing the collective power of those around us to keep up. That has implications for how we collaborate and how we open our doors to other organizations, an approach that is often called 'open innovation'.

What does that mean for companies? It means they must also work hard to stay relevant. Jack Welch, the former GE CEO, said, unless the rate of change within the company matches the rate of change outside the company, the end is near. Essentially, everything we will discuss over the next few sections is about trying to find ways of keeping that gap under control.

Third, change is messy. If you pick up any book or article about change management, you will see a shocking statistic: 70 per cent of change programmes fail. We can debate how accurate this figure is,[4] but it suggests a huge range of outcomes and also indicates how hard it is to know – ultimately – whether any given change programme achieved its objectives. Indeed, we would note that change programmes should not be evaluated in a binary way. They typically work to *some* degree – there's always something positive that comes out of such a programme. There may be some failures or missteps along the way, but good leaders adapt, they keep pushing and orienting things in the right direction and they find a way to move forward. Change programmes do not just succeed or fail.

In this section, we will delve into what the digital specific aspects of change are. There are plenty of well-known generic articles on change and transformation. For example, there's a well-known framework by John Kotter, who came up with an eight-step guide on how to manage change.[5] Kotter talks about setting the direction first, then he talks about engaging and enabling people and then embedding the process. It is well worth looking at his and other people's research in this area, but our focus in this chapter is on managing the *digital* aspects of change programmes.

CHANGE IN A DIGITAL CONTEXT: THE UK'S GOVERNMENT DIGITAL SERVICE

Let's consider the process of change either as a chief executive or senior executive who is trying to map out a strategy, a programme of where they want to go and how they will get there. There's a framework by A.G. Lafley, former Chief Executive of Procter & Gamble, and Roger Martin, the former Dean of Rotman Business School, in their book, *Playing to Win*. The framework is possibly the most widely used framework for strategy deployment in use today.[6]

There are five steps, which you can picture as a cascade from left to right: Step 1, define a winning aspiration; Step 2, figure out where to play, what markets and product areas are you going to serve?; Step 3, figure out how you will win, what your positioning will be against competitors in those markets; Step 4, develop the necessary capabilities to do that; Step 5, build the management systems to support them. It's a linear process, each one following on logically from the other.

Although this is a widely used framework, its rational, linear structure limits its suitability to the fast-paced world today. If you reflect on the shift from so-called 'waterfall' to 'agile' development in software (discussed in Chapter 4, *see also* page 79), you can make a similar case here that the Lafley and Martin strategy change programme is not iterative or fluid enough.

Here is a detailed example to help build this argument.

Mike Bracken was the executive director of the UK Government Digital Service (GDS) from 2011 to 2014, during which time he led a transformation of the UK's public sector's online services.[7] And by all accounts, it was a huge success. The *Washington Post* hailed it as the 'gold standard of digital government' and according to an international comparative analysis, the UK was best-in-world in terms of the quality of its digital service in 2016 (though it subsequently fell in these rankings after Bracken's departure).[8]

The UK government had pursued a series of fragmented and tentative digital initiatives in the 1990s and 2000s, but this changed in 2011 when GDS was formed as a small team within the Cabinet Office under the Cabinet Minister, Francis Maude. Mike Bracken, former chief digital officer at the *Guardian* newspaper, was hired to lead the team. He recognized the enormity of the challenge as it would involve cajoling dozens of government departments he had no direct control over to adopt a common set of standards and principles in creating digital services. His initial 'asks' of Francis Maude were to have full control of the www.gov.uk website, plus freedom to choose his own team and to operate in his own distinctive way. He rented office space a mile away from the main government departments in central London to give him the space he needed.

Rather than put together a detailed top-down change programme, Bracken started small, using agile prototyping principles, such as 'show don't tell' and 'start with user needs'. His team built a prototype website to give government departments a feel for what they wanted to achieve and then they took on whatever was offered to them – for example, an e-petitions project. Gradually, they built up some momentum and gained credibility for rapid and effective delivery in some departments. Their priorities were to 'fix publishing', which meant getting all online documents up to an acceptable and common set of standards, then 'fix transactions', which referred to the most common things people needed to do, such as renew their driving licence or apply for a passport. Finally, they planned to 'go whole-sale' by opening up data through Application Programme interfaces (APIs) so that private sector organizations could build user-centric applications on top of centrally-held data.

Bracken's emphasis on user-centred design and small-team delivery worked extremely well. GDS won the UK's Design of the Year award in 2013 for www.gov.uk and by 2014, it had achieved its goals of fixing publishing and transactions across all the major government departments. He continued to face significant resistance in the form of department heads preferring to do things their own way and seeking to marginalize his small central team but throughout the process he stayed true to his mantra, *The Strategy is Delivery*. This meant focusing first and foremost on getting things done – operating on a sufficiently fast cycle time that they could cut through opposition by showing immediate results. It also meant not writing lengthy policy proposals that needed buy-in in advance. Bracken's director of policy summarized the challenge as follows:

> *Whitehall alone has around 17,000 professionals with policy in their title: traditionally, they have understood an important part of their job as writing the requirements which someone else has to implement. This creates the implementation gap we see so often in the public sector. Our approach, based around control of the gov.uk domain, has allowed us to get a lot of things done very quickly and to show how things can be done.*

In summary, Mike Bracken's change programme at GDS was all about doing, not planning. His first priority was to have the freedom to act – with physical separation from Whitehall (the offices of the UK government), his own commercially-minded people and control of the www.gov.uk domain. His second priority was to gain high-level support, which Francis Maude duly provided. His third priority was to start getting things done, as captured in his tagline 'the strategy is delivery'. For the 17,000 policymaking professionals mentioned above, there was an implicit view that they needed to write papers and build buy-in before doing anything. Bracken's view was that if GDS had fallen into the trap of writing papers and asking for support, they would have been killed at birth. 'The last thing we are ever going to do is write documents,' he said. 'Our job is to deliver and prove our existence by what we **do**, not what we **say** we are going to do.'

Bracken's approach was to take action within a broadly defined mandate, see what works and then make sense of the emerging strategy as they went along. By contrast, the classic waterfall approach to software programming, or the Lafley and Martin framework described above, focuses on a more rigid and linear set of decisions based on the output of the previous step.

Now, which is the right model? Of course, the answer is it depends on the circumstances, neither is right or wrong as such. However, the Agile approach to strategy execution works much better in the fast-changing digital environment most businesses find themselves operating in today and we would certainly encourage you to think – and act – this way.

THE ROLE OF THE LEADER

What is the role of the leader in a digital transformation? Well, clearly, it is to lead and drive the change process. If you consider Mike Bracken's story, or the changes John made at Pearson, you see a clear sense of purpose and direction in terms of where they're going and what they're trying to achieve. In the process, this enables them to put in place the right coalition of people to manage the process and support them along the way.

One interesting way of framing the new role of the leader is to go back to the three organizing models – bureaucracy, meritocracy and adhocracy – that we talked about in Chapter 4 (*see also* page 90). The leader has a subtly different role in each of these three models.

Take the bureaucracy, where the emphasis is on efficiency and productivity. The role of a leader in making a bureaucratic process work, and indeed in changing a bureaucratic process, can be relatively top-down in nature. There is typically a high level of clarity in what you are aiming for and a clarity of roles and responsibilities all the way down, so that the leader can ensure everybody does what is agreed.

If we consider the meritocracy, the leader still has formal authority but he or she generates legitimacy through expertise and judgement, and typically leads through a process of negotiation and discussion that seeks to get to the right answer. It's a more involved process of leadership where nothing is pushed down without a conversation. In this situation, the leader derives his or her authority largely because they have genuine expertise themselves and are very good at handling conversations and managing the flow of information up, down and sideways.

In an adhocracy, making things happen is the priority, as we saw in the Mike Bracken story. In such a setting, the leader needs a clear sense of what the organization is trying to achieve and what success might look like, but he or she is typically fuzzier on the details of how to arrive at the final destination than in a bureaucracy or meritocracy. While some time might be spent developing a vision, more time is spent working with the people below, energizing them, giving them the freedom to act, giving them the responsibility to essentially fill in all the gaps in the strategy between today and tomorrow. It's a much more enabling form of leadership.

How does this framework apply to John's experience at Pearson?

We made decisions where a somewhat top-down style was necessary. For example, when considering selling the Financial Times, *we understood that once it was sold, it could not be unsold. I made sure that all the right senior colleagues at the* FT *were involved and consulted, but, ultimately, it was a decision that only the board could make. Implementing a new enterprise resource system, moving the company to the Cloud, moving our textbook's business from a print to digital-first model… each of these were decisions that were both the sum of thousands of previous iterative decisions but also that, once made, could not be unwound without huge strategic pain. Each of these decisions required a necessary degree of rigour. Lots of colleagues were engaged in the decision-making process and you listen to what they think and feel, but, ultimately, these are the decisions that only a CEO, working with their executive team and board, can take.*

To be sure, some of these decisions were not popular. For example, once we decided the whole company was going to implement a new platform, many people would complain that the platform chosen was not the one they wanted, was not in line with their bespoke requirements and that they didn't want to give up the systems they were used to. In that instance, once we were confident that after listening to all perspectives, we were doing what was best for the company overall, we had to hold the line and effectively tell colleagues to get on with it. In these and other cases, a combination of bureaucracy (process and rules) and meritocracy (logical argument) was the right way forward.

However, if the question is around the need to innovate and iterate, to create new products and services for our customer's changing needs, then the leader effectively must grant a licence to colleagues to explore. For example, at Pearson, one of our fastest-growing businesses, our virtual schools business, shifted one summer from having a very traditional TV-based marketing campaign to making much greater use of social media and a more data-rich message around learning outcomes rather than a softer, warmer feeling about parental piece of mind. It didn't land well, and we had to revert back quickly, but not without some lost business and financial pain.

Now, at the executive level, we hadn't been involved – quite rightly – in any of the decision making. We only became aware of the problem when enrolment numbers were tracking well below where we expected. We met with the business unit to understand and dissect what had happened, but not in a spirit of blame or to hang anyone out to dry. The marketing team had chosen to move quickly in an agile manner and created a campaign that was in line with the strategy. Okay, they had not trialled the campaign or sought external feedback first in the way they might have done. But the sole purpose of the meeting was: what did we learn? What insights have we gained that can help us to be better next time?

In the process, we started to tell that story around the company. We were not 'celebrating' the failure, but we were acknowledging that for the people who tried and did the right things in line with the strategy, the learnings and action points actually gave us deeper insights for the future. And that's when people started to realize that it was okay to innovate and not always succeed – as long as we responded quickly and learnt from the experience.

Jeremy Darroch of Sky made a similar point to us, the idea of not being riskless but not being reckless either:

> *There cannot be any comparison between bidding for Premier League football over a weekend in a blind auction versus some digital innovation. Those are just entirely different things. Part of the discipline of being a leader and being further up the organization is understanding the importance of doing the work that you have to do as opposed to necessarily what you might want to do. It is very easy to get involved in a lot of stuff that's attractive and interesting but actually, there's lots more people in the organization better enabled to get on with our work. So what you need to do is just let them get on with it. Commit your time to higher-order or one-way decisions that you've got to get right.*

In the next part of this chapter, we look at aspects of the change process in more detail, separating out the internal challenge (i.e. employees of the company) from the external challenge (customers, suppliers, analysts, shareholders and the like). Then we finish with some advice to you in whatever role you have, whether you are in a leadership position or in a middle-manager role.

THE INTERNAL PROCESS OF CHANGE

Managing the process of change with internal stakeholders, whether it's an organization of 50,000 people, or 50 people, is all about orienting them towards the long-term intended transformation. But in our experience, regardless of how well thought-out and necessary the change is, there will always be internal resistance and the process of gaining the necessary buy-in will always be longer and more difficult than you envision at the start. Coram Williams shared this reflection from his experiences across several companies:

> *What has surprised me each time I've been through a transformation has been the internal level of scepticism about why this has to happen, whether it's being done correctly, and quite often, personal attacks*

on the leaders and what their motivation is. Really as a leader, dig deep, be clear on why this has to happen and why it's important. This requires a huge level of resilience and being able to put one's ego to one side.

Here is an example of a change programme in a digital business. It's the story of **Refinitiv**, which was spun out of information services giant Thomson Reuters in 2018 under David Craig's leadership.[9] By way of background, Thomson Reuters (TR) was formed in 2008 through the acquisition of the London-based Reuters Group by the Toronto-based and family-controlled Thomson Corporation. TR operated across four areas of business information, the largest of which was the Financial & Risk (F&R) division led by David Craig. This division was facing a difficult market situation, given the increasing focus on regulation and compliance following the financial crisis, and increasing competition from Bloomberg. Craig led a major restructuring in 2012, simplifying the product portfolio, reducing products from 800 to under 200, and cutting 3,000 jobs, resulting in $300 million in cost savings.

By 2016, F&R showed signs of improvements in its margins (though revenue growth had stalled). However, Craig felt he was being held back by the TR corporate board, who were not providing the level of investment or urgency needed. He took the risky decision to propose a carve-out – whereby his division would operate as an independent business with external investment. Following discussions with the Blackstone Group in 2017, this carve-out model was agreed. Craig would run the F&R business under the name Refinitiv, majority owned by Blackstone, and TR would retain control of the remaining businesses in science, legal and accounting information. This new structure, which came into operation in 2018, gave Refinitiv access to the investment it needed to thrive in the fast-evolving financial data industry.

In the period 2018–20, David Craig led Refinitiv through a major process of internal change as it sought to establish itself as an independent company. He targeted $650 million in savings,

3–5 per cent annual growth and operating margins in the high 30s. Craig focused on customer-centricity, resulting in improved customer satisfaction and renewals. Structural changes included an IPO for the Tradeweb trading platform and several acquisitions. Employee motivation increased through a revamped rewards structure and a development program called 'Leadershift' enhanced leadership values.

One specific point here was shifting away from a generic bonus scheme to one where some people received twice their salary as bonus and others almost no bonus at all. To make this possible, he changed the rating scale from a five-point to a four-point evaluation scale, thus forcing managers to evaluate individuals as either above average or below average, but never average. This allowed him to make some tough choices about the types of people and the types of motivation and effort he was getting from his employees and enabled the culture change.

These changes contributed to improved financial performance, with annual sales growth of 2.6 per cent in 2018 and 2019 and an increased EBITDA margin of 35 per cent. The company also shifted its emphasis in product development, adopting a horizontal 'platform' model for data and analytics operations. In 2020, Refinitiv was acquired by the London Stock Exchange Group (LSEG) for a premium of $6 billion over the value of Refinitiv when it was carved out of TR three years earlier. At the time of writing, in 2024, the acquisition appeared successful, with Refinitiv continuing to generate growth in revenue and profit in a highly competitive market.

What are the lessons from Refinitiv? One key point we would make is the importance of a clear sense of purpose in enabling change. There was an explicit starting point (January 2018) when the company came into existence and a strong desire among employees to forge their own identity, after years of feeling like an oppressed division of Thomson Reuters. There was also a clearly defined battleground, with Bloomberg as its biggest competitor and a looming threat from digital giants like Google. The Refinitiv's purpose statement, 'advancing together beyond the speed of change', spoke of the importance of nimbleness in a rapidly changing market and it was something the employees could get behind.

It is also useful to note just how hard David Craig and his team worked on managing the change process. The nitty-gritty details are often brushed over in historical accounts of successful change programmes, but there should be no illusions about what's involved. By way of example, here are Annette Thomas's reflections on leading a major programme of change at Macmillan Publishing:

> *I was looking at this big transformation, where we were looking at merging the 75 companies in the group, into three larger groups. Initially, we believed it would take six months, but gradually we grew to understand that for an organization with 5,000–6,000 staff in 150 countries, six months would become three years.*
>
> *As we got into the weeds of it, we realized just how much we had missed. Where are we today and where do we want to be and how exactly are we going to get there? Who's going to do what? How is the operating model going to change? How is this going to impact on people? How are the skill sets going to change over time? How are we going to do that? That's one of the hardest challenges.*
>
> *Most importantly, what I learned was that there's two fundamental members of the team that you absolutely need as you start this journey. One is an amazing chief people officer and the other is an impactful chief communications officer, because you need to be able to have support. Thinking through each of these questions and gaining people support for the transformation we were undertaking was absolutely critical.*

SUMMARIZING THE CHANGE PROCESS

We have mentioned Pearson, Refinitiv, Macmillan Publishing and the UK's Government Digital Service as examples of change programmes in largely digital organizational settings. We could share many more similar stories and of course readers will have their own favourite examples as well. To be clear, we aren't suggesting that a 'digital' change process is fundamentally different to an 'industrial' change process, as there are many aspects that apply in all settings. Rather, we believe the challenges you face as a leader are particularly acute in terms of the pace of change and transparency needed in the process and the importance of bottom-up involvement. Here in summary are the five hallmarks of an effective internal change process:

1. *Clear purpose.* Every organization has a set of pre-existing routines, practises, ways of working that are difficult to shift away from. As social psychologist Kurt Lewin first observed, you typically need to 'unfreeze' an organization before you can make it change. Unfreezing sometimes comes through acknowledging a crisis, a burning platform. It can also come from articulating a higher ambition. Whichever path you choose, this purpose must be front-and-centre in all your communications.

2. *Getting buy-in from employees.* The problem is often not that employees are actively against what you're trying to do (unless their own livelihoods are at stake). For the most part, they are disinterested. They have their own priorities and do not spend enormous amounts of time thinking about the messaging that you are sending from above. You need to use multiple lines of persuasion. Some people respond well to logical and rational arguments. Others (and it's probably the majority) are looking for arguments with some emotional resonance, so they can understand what's in it for them.[10]

3. *A bias for action.* As individuals, we have habits; ingrained personal day-to-day routines that are actually quite difficult to break. To overcome such habits, we have to move towards a discipline of encouraging experimentation. This has been a theme throughout the book – for example, it's a key feature of the model of organizing we call adhocracy. One of the overarching aims in a change programme is putting people in a position where they feel encouraged to try out something new to see if it works, for them to reflect on it and hopefully use it as an impetus for doing more.

4. *A supportive culture.* Many organizations have what's called a 'blame' culture – when something doesn't work out, you point the finger at someone or something else. The alternative, which is something we have been alluding to throughout this book, is an environment of psychological safety, one in which people feel free to try things out and are not fearful that they will be punished when something goes awry. Well-intentioned failure is acceptable and even to some degree promoted – as long as you learn from it and act quickly on what you have learnt – as John's example above illustrated.

5. *An enabling structure.* We have talked at length about how bureaucracy stifles initiative and slows things down. A good enabling structure is one that keeps the amount of structure around people as light as possible. We saw this in the Refinitiv case study, where David Craig did a lot of work around delayering and empowering employees and giving them access to the information to help them make better decisions themselves.

Each of these five dimensions will have varying degrees of influence, but collectively, are pivotal in the change process. As you think through your own company, reflect on which of these dimensions are already working well and which you struggle with and how you might overcome those challenges.

BRINGING EXTERNAL STAKEHOLDERS ALONG ON THE JOURNEY

As we have noted several times in the book, publicly traded companies such as Pearson face a special kind of challenge during a period of disruption. They must compete with startups who, at least initially, are typically judged by their venture capital backers based on top-line growth rather than profitability, and they must meet the need of their own shareholders who, as Patrick Wellington told us, 'want everything. They want growth, they want margin, and they want durability.'

It's a not an easy trick to pull off. Here are John's reflections on this period:

What was quite unusual was that we went through this hugely disruptive analogue-to-digital transformation while remaining a public company. Our major competitors went through several private equity owners over this period. One of them filed for chapter 11 bankruptcy, with debts of over $4 billion. If you look at the music industry, which went through something similar in terms of its scale and impact, none of the big music companies stayed public throughout the digital disruption of their industry.

The shareholders that are attracted to investing in large-scale incumbents are mostly those investing money on behalf of pension funds and therefore are dependent on dividends. For them, visibility, and predictability to deliver financial results in three, six, 12 months is important. An analogue-to-digital transformation is disruptive and means you really cannot predict what will happen in the short term. We did consider whether it would be better to seek support from private equity or venture capital, but each of these sources of capital provided their own challenges. We stuck to staying public, while spending an enormous amount of time with our shareholder base communicating our story, sharing with them, alongside the financial results, key performance indicators on digital progress and asking that they trust and stick with us.

We also had to manage our other external stakeholders, including ministries of education, government departments, universities and large corporations, all of whom were important customers for us. They too were worried, seeing the press reports of profits warnings, and wondered about the financial viability of the business. We again spent time reassuring them that our commitment to enabling people to progress in their lives through education and learning was rock solid and if anything, would be enhanced by pursuing and completing our transformation. We tried to build an alliance with our external stakeholders so they saw that we had a clear purpose as a company and shared our long-term vision.

Pearson's Coram Williams shared his perspective on why digital change is so challenging for publicly-traded companies:

> *Many public markets investors prize consistency, predictability and steady revenue and earnings growth. If you look at the companies that they value, they have to be able to look at it, model it and know that when they look back at that model in 12 months' time, the company has delivered. The problem with digital transitions is that they fundamentally take away the consistency of the business because you've got models and businesses shifting and at different trajectories. The predictability is very difficult because they're not linear and everything that the market wants, digital transitions work against.*

Patrick Wellington, Vice Chairman of Rothschild & Co., has seen a similar story play out across a wide range of media companies. He reminded us that it is important to understand how an investment fund manager thinks about the world and your company:

> *A fund manager's job is to worry about everything and to be excited about everything. Their job is to say, 'I own this company, I've got a thesis about this company. What's the transformational change on the horizon which might affect the business? Is that actually going to emerge as a threat? At what point do I need to worry about that? At what point is that going to impinge on what might be a perfectly well performing company at the moment?' They worry about it the other way round. 'Is this company much better than I thought? Are the prospects vastly better than I thought? Should I own twice as much of this company as I actually do?' You're constantly as a fund manager trying to look over the horizon and think, where might this change? What might go wrong, and when is that going to impact me?*

Patrick has spent a lot of time with company management teams, as well as fund managers, so he is well qualified to describe the challenges they in turn face – and why a good management team grappling with the potential threat of digital disruption should see the investment community as another valuable source of market insight as well as of all important financial capital:

This is a very difficult environment for managers to deal with because they may be looking at their business at that moment and think well, the business is running perfectly well. We've got tremendous incumbent strengths, we're running the business very well, we're very efficient. Yet their shareholders suddenly set them a different exam question: you've got to deal with what we perceive to be a disruptive force coming over the horizon. Fund managers are very smart and they have access to masses of information. They can go anywhere in the world to virtually any company and look at any trend. Often they will detect things which the company management may not have. You're busy running a business. What they do is find out information and look at trends.

So, what's our advice to companies who are facing this type of disruptive threat in engaging with their shareholders?

Take professional advice. Never, ever communicate with the financial markets without first taking professional advice. There are very strict rules regarding financial disclosure and how companies communicate externally on their financial performance and commercial prospects. Your company will almost certainly have an in-house investor relations function and external advisers. Make sure you work closely with them and take their advice.

Be clear and straightforward in your communication with the markets. While it's human nature to try to hedge yourself when facing difficult circumstances, it's important to remember that the analysts and institutional investors – the people who have the biggest influence on your share price – are experts in interpreting and decoding your language. Here are the reflections of Patrick Wellington:

One of the things that the market hates is uncertainty. You must be very careful about your language as people will pick up on everything that you say and on what you don't say. They look for subliminal messages to see whether you look happy, confident or whether you look nervy and uncomfortable. I remember once being on the phone to a CFO and he cut away and said, 'It's like pushing water up a hill.' Instantly I thought, 'his is not a happy company'.

Another pet hate of mine is a CEO using the word 'broadly'. If something is starting to go wrong, many CEOs will say that the business is 'broadly flat'. This effectively encourages the market to take the worst assumption. You must be very clear about your messaging.

Accept that sometimes it's going to be a long haul. It's human nature to monitor your share price and to see its value as a vote of confidence (or not) in you as a leadership team. But shareholders and analysts are playing their own game and it's one you have limited influence over. As Patrick Wellington observed:

One should never take a share price personally. If shareholders remain unconvinced that within ten years, there is the hint of an emergent threat that will wipe out your business and management are unaware of or unsure of how to counter it, the company share price will reflect that almost immediately. There is no staged development and that then becomes the norm from which your valuation is based. It does not matter how well you run your company. Until you can disprove that existential threat over the duration of time, or until you can fully transition your business, the share price will reflect those concerns.

Keep highlighting the strengths of the business. If you are a music company, highlight the fact that you have content people love and share some of the positive metrics. If you are an education business, remind your audience that you have high-quality material that has been regulated, reviewed and is sellable in a way that competitors cannot match. If one business division is going through a difficult transition, remind them of the other parts of the company that are performing well. Although the ultimate measure of success will be growing sales, profits and cash generation, you can point shareholders to other means of tracking progress in your digital transition in the interim – such as digital registrations, take up of new digital products, Net Promoter Scores, and the percentage of group revenues coming from digital products or services.

Manage the company's balance sheet to ensure you have the financial strength to weather the storm. We noted in chapter two that Pearson used the proceeds from the asset sales of its newspaper and trade publishing businesses to pay down debt. This meant that, in a period when borrowing money was cheap, Pearson was running what the capital markets would normally consider an inefficient balance sheet. But this fiscally conservative approach was appreciated by its shareholders, in the context of the wider challenges faced by the company. As Patrick Wellington puts it:

> I used to say that whatever else you think about Pearson, they're going to be around at the end of this process because the balance sheet is absolutely fine. You can take a view on how many years it's going to take the College business to make this physical to digital transition, or argue about whether it is ever going to happen. But there are other businesses within Pearson which are actually very solid and the company will emerge on the other side because it's got a perfectly good, strong balance sheet.

Consider a different governance structure. As we noted earlier, even though Pearson – and its shareholders – chose to remain a public company, listed on the London Stock Exchange, many of its competitors went private. Sometimes this shift in ownership is forced on a public company when it faces the risk of bankruptcy, sometimes it happens because a private equity company sees an opportunity to buy out an undervalued asset, turn it around or break it up, and then sell on the assets for a premium later.

Why does the governance structure of the business matter when you're going through a major transformation? Key variables to keep in mind are the risk appetite of your owners and your access to funding. While publicly traded companies have many long-term investors, there are short-term buyers and sellers who often make a lot of noise and whose views can shape the entire narrative about your prospects. In contrast, privately held companies, whether they are part of a big private equity group like Blackstone, or owned by a family or a sovereign government, can stay out of the spotlight. Their investors are comfortable with the risks they are taking and typically have a time horizon of at least five years.

Access to capital is the other big factor. There was a time when being publicly traded gave you preferential access to the equity and debt markets than being held privately, but that has changed with the spectacular growth in the amount of private capital available for investment. Indeed, as we saw with Refinitiv, going private was in fact a more effective way of accessing capital than remaining a listed entity. On the other hand, partnerships, as we often see in professional services, are not structured to take on large amounts of debt so even though they avoid the vagaries of stock market valuations, their ability to make big investments through a transformation programme is limited.

Stick with it. However hard the going gets and no matter how long it takes, do not be distracted; do not be deterred. Recognize that sometimes the circumstances choose you and all you can do is act in what you believe to be the best long-term interests of the company. Here is Coram Williams' final reflection on the Pearson transformation:

> *What worked at Pearson was that John had a very clear perspective as to why Pearson had a right to exist and herein lies the lesson. The resilience comes in strong part from that unyielding sense of purpose or belief that the very reason the company exists is because it matters – you have to have a very clear compass, which is guiding you in terms of why you're doing what you're doing and why it's the right thing. Only then can you dig deep.*

INNOVATING FROM WHERE YOU ARE: TOP-DOWN VERSUS MIDDLE-UP

Throughout this chapter, we have focused on the CEO and the senior leadership as the individuals with ultimate responsibility for the digital transformation process but for readers in mid to senior positions, it is useful to think about your role in the change. What can you do to shape things for the better in your part of the organization? And how can you be a useful contributor to the programme of change that is being led from the top? Here are three areas you should be working on.

The first is a general deepening and broadening of your understanding of the new business environment. It's easy to be bamboozled by new technologies, or to be intimidated by the threat of disruption. The more knowledgeable you are, the more you can push back with smart questions and cautionary tales from other industries. You can become an important contributor to the collective decision-making process in your organization and you can make smarter decisions yourself in the areas of the business you have control over.

The second is to become a proactive influencer, where you bring new opportunities to the attention of top management. Every organization has its own norms about how to do this, so it's hard to be prescriptive. You might seek time in a management meeting, workshop or away-day to bring people up to speed on a new technology. You might have a Slack channel or knowledge community where like-minded people share their ideas. You might be invited to participate in a training programme where people work together on business projects. There may even be an opportunity to pitch a senior executive directly.

The third is to pursue an opportunity directly. We often refer to this as corporate entrepreneurship (or intrapreneurship), in that it involves working with others inside and sometimes outside the organization, typically without any sort of formal mandate, with a view to developing something out of nothing. Many large companies are ambivalent about corporate entrepreneurship because it seems to condone the maverick-like behaviours that can sometimes get them into trouble. Here is how John thought about this at Pearson:

We did not want people running around, trying to decide which enterprise resource planning system to use, or telling us which businesses we should sell or acquire. For these sorts of decisions, you really need proper systems and processes. But there are times, when dealing directly with customers, when you should empower front-line staff to ask for forgiveness rather than permission. One of our regional sales managers had an account with a major university, and using her own initiative, went to the senior leadership of the university and said, 'You are using all these different Pearson courses; if you can guarantee a higher sell-through on the digital product, I can probably negotiate a discount for you.' That broke every rule we had on pricing. But she then went to her boss and said, 'Look, if I can get this done, will you do it?' Her boss said, 'Yes, I'll support it.' It was this idea that led us to create the inclusive access model, a vital plank of our shift from our old model of customers owning single-line products to a subscription model, with access to multiple products. So, in dealing directly with customers, you do need to trust and empower your people to do the right thing in the moment – and then have the formal and informal feedback loops by which you can learn from them.

The reason the inclusive access model worked was because it wasn't created in a corporate event of some kind, but rather a salesperson responding to a very real customer need in the flow of her job. That is where all the best innovation tends to happen, understanding pain point signals from the customer and responding quickly to that need.

In sum, large organizations like Pearson have no shortage of potentially interesting ideas bubbling up from below. It's important for senior leaders to clarify what are the big themes to focus on, that they are interested in tapping into – and for people at all levels of the company to be passionate and persuasive at how they are dealing with them with their specific customers.

SOME CONCLUDING THOUGHTS

We noted at the outset of this chapter that it can be lonely at the top. The leader is surrounded by colleagues, employees, board members and advisors, yet when it comes to the big decisions, they find themselves shouldering the burden largely alone. We also talked about huge challenges leaders must face when working through a major process of change. With the exponential growth and adoption of AI in every aspect of our lives – which we discuss in the next chapter – these challenges are only going to become ever more acute for more companies.

7

How Might ChatGPT Change the World?

We have talked about ChatGPT and Generative AI intermittently throughout the book but it deserves a chapter of its own. While every new technology brings fresh challenges and opportunities, we note two key themes in this book: first, the impact of new technology tends to be overhyped in the short term but underestimated over time; second, if you look at previous waves of technology, you can discern common ideas – an emergent playbook – that shapes how incumbents adapt to survive in the new world order. We think there is good reason to believe that both these themes will hold true in the age of AI.

INVESTING IN AI APPLICATIONS IN PEARSON

The past is a useful guide to the future. As Mark Twain said, history may not repeat itself, but it certainly rhymes. Here is John's account of an earlier attempt to apply AI in the business he led:

In late October 2016, my colleague, Tim Bozik, Pearson's President of Global Product, took to the stage in Las Vegas, where 17,000 business executives from all over the world had gathered for IBM's World of Watson event. Ever since Watson – IBM's branding of its data ingestion and machine-learning capabilities that could answer questions posed in natural language – had beaten the very best human players on the American TV quiz show, Jeopardy, the company had been marketing aggressively that it was ready to transform the world of business, with healthcare and education at the forefront.

Tim was there to launch a new global education alliance, between IBM and Pearson, that would make Watson's AI-driven capabilities available to millions of college professors and students. The big idea was to embed an intelligent teaching assistant, powered by Watson, into Pearson's digital courseware. Watson would already have read the Pearson courseware and be ready to spot patterns and generate insights. The intelligent teaching assistant would, in real time, assess the student's response, guide them with hints, feedback, explanations, answer their questions and help identify common misconceptions. It would work with students at their own pace, to help them master the topic.

This idea of an adaptive learning system delivering personalized education was not new. As Audrey Watters recounts in her book, Teaching Machines,[1] education technologists had been pursuing a similar vision since the 1920s. More recently, pioneering use of machine learning and natural language processing had helped Pearson build its world leading professional certification business, by delivering computer-based testing that was far more secure, flexible and reliable than tests set and scored by humans. Over 10 million college students a year were using AI-inspired tools that automated the setting and marking of homework, as we've described in earlier chapters. But these were more limited in scope, using multiple choice and fill in the blank questions that offered only a partial view of student understanding. What Pearson and IBM were announcing in Las Vegas promised to be a major advance on that. This was machine-driven cognitive learning, a flexible virtual tutor, powered by artificial intelligence.

Sadly, the reality never lived up to the advanced publicity. Despite a huge amount of work by the IBM and Pearson teams, we could never quite create a product that would deliver on our ambitions for it – and our global education alliance ended some 18 months later.

Pearson wasn't the only company that jumped on the AI bandwagon too early. For example, IBM sought to use Watson to revolutionize cancer treatment in partnership with the MD Anderson Cancer Center in Houston in 2013. Called Oncology Expert Advisor, it sought to create a bedside diagnostic tool, but after four years and $62 million worth of investment, it was shut down. According to one observer, 'Instead of being a shorthand for technological prowess, Watson stands out as a sobering example of the pitfalls of technological hype and hubris around AI.'[2] And it's not just IBM that overestimated the potential of AI over the last decade – in their different ways, Alphabet/Google, Meta/Facebook, Tesla and Amazon have all been guilty of promising more than they could deliver.

But times change, and AI gets better all the time.

Seven years on from Pearson's ill-fated partnership with IBM, there is renewed excitement in the world of education that, with the huge breakthroughs made in generative AI by OpenAI and others, the age of truly adaptive, personalized learning is finally with us. The most common use case – adaptive chatbots as intelligent reading partners that ask students questions, interpret their answers and provide feedback during study – sounds very similar to what Pearson was trying to achieve with IBM Watson. In late 2023, Pearson itself started introducing generative AI into its e-textbooks and is now expanding the rollout to many more titles.

We spoke to Tim Bozik and another former Pearson executive, John Behrens, about the Pearson/IBM Watson project, to see what lessons might have been learnt. Behrens observed just how dramatically the technology has improved since then:

We had to train Watson how to categorize every single sentence of student responses. Current models do that on the fly, along with millions of other computational tasks automatically. If you think about GPT 4 having 175 billion parameters estimated simultaneously, with Watson, we were probably making 100 or so specific parameters (per question/answer pair) at a time. We were making best in class propeller planes, then the jet engine came along.

Tim Bozik's view was more equivocal:

> *I'm not sure if the Watson tutor was ahead of its time and limited by IBM's technology, not focused on the right use-cases, or overly ambitious and generalized; it was probably a combination of these factors.*

One lesson, he noted, was that universities and publishers should take '*a decentralized test-and-learn approach, as a means to discover what works and doesn't in situ*', something we have been endorsing frequently throughout the book.

We will return to the views of Tim Bozik and John Behrens, and how they resonate with many of our earlier arguments, towards the end of the chapter but let's first take a step back, with an overview of why ChatGPT has made such a huge impact on the business world.

THE FIRST CONSUMER-ORIENTED AI PRODUCT

The launch of ChatGPT in November 2022 brought long-standing technical discussions of the potential of AI into the public discourse. For the first time ever, people around the world had instant access to AI. They didn't need any advanced IT skills, or any understanding of how the technology works, they simply used it and marvelled at what it came up with.

The obvious comparison, in terms of historical precedent, is the World Wide Web, created in 1993 by Tim Berners-Lee. This invention turned the internet – an obscure system linking up researchers and university scientists around the world – into something consumers across the globe could access. Thanks to ChatGPT, AI is now a consumer product in its own right, creating enormous opportunities but also significant challenges.

There are some obvious consequences when you put AI in the hands of millions of consumers around the world. First, awareness and usage increase exponentially, opening up ways of applying the technology that its inventors could never have dreamt of. Second, commercial interests take over, with big-tech and startup companies leading the way in exploiting the technology for commercial advantage. Third, the limitations of the technology are exposed, sparking a useful debate about risks and biases. Regulation and oversight – some useful, some burdensome – quickly follow.

All of these things are now playing out. The invention of the World Wide Web in 1993 kicked off the internet revolution, the emergence of Amazon, Google and Facebook and others; and the reinvention of Microsoft and Apple. As the consumerization of AI takes off, we will see some new players emerge (like OpenAI and Anthropic), though we can expect the big-tech players to retain their dominance in many respects. Indeed, one of the features of the AI era is that many of these new players – such as OpenAI and Anthropic – are aligned with, and funded by, Big Tech.

There will also be as-yet unforeseeable opportunities. Consider the analogy to the internet, where our openness to sharing information about ourselves and our intentions online created what author Shoshana Zuboff calls a 'behavioural surplus', which was then exploited by Google and Facebook through paid ads.[3] What new behaviours will we develop, as we increasingly use ChatGPT and other GPTs to help us with our everyday lives, that entrepreneurs might harness for their own benefit? What new 'killer apps' will emerge to disrupt existing sectors? Great riches await those that come up with the best answers to these questions.

One thing is for sure – the arrival of AI as a consumer product isn't the end of the story, it's actually just the inflection point that heralds even more change, as the underlying technology continues to improve and as new possibilities come into focus. For example, in July 2023, Mustafa Suleyman, one of the founders of Google DeepMind, called for a new 'Turing Test'. You might recall the original one, named after Alan Turing, an AI pioneer from the 1950s. It was based on a simple language conversation between two invisible partners. If the observer couldn't figure out which was the computer and which was the human, then the computer passed the test.

Suleyman said that in terms of text conversation (and indeed many other skills such as voice and image recognition), AI has already passed the Turing Test, so we need to raise the bar. It's not enough for AI to be able to process and generate information – it needs to show what it can do. He says:

> To pass the Modern Turing Test, an AI would have to successfully act on this instruction: 'Go make $1 million on a retail web platform in a few months with just a $100,000 investment.'[4]

Clearly this is a big ask – it would require the AI to design a new product, work with manufacturers, come up with marketing campaigns and so forth. Our view, as discussed below, is that some of these tasks may be forever beyond the realms of possibility but the point is, if one of the leaders in AI is already talking in these terms, we should take the challenge seriously. If AI is moving from the world of thought to the world of action, there are important consequences for all of us.

In the rest of the chapter, we will explore some of the immediate and longer-term consequences of AI for the world of business. We certainly don't have all the answers, but based on our recent experiences, and on the lessons from this book, we can provide a sense of direction and we can put forward some hopefully useful provocations.

GENERATIVE AI – WHAT DOES IT DO?

Most people have no idea how AI works. As the writer Arthur C. Clarke famously said, 'Any sufficiently advanced technology is indistinguishable from magic.' And this is certainly the case with ChatGPT, which astounds most users when they first try it out.

So, a couple of points of introduction for those unfamiliar with the technology. (Here, we will focus on ChatGPT because it's the most well-used application, but there are many similar products and many other forms of Generative AI.)[5] First, ChatGPT does not think or understand in the way a human does. It has an algorithm (a model) that takes the question you have asked it and it generates a string of words in response by interrogating the enormous body of data (from the internet) that it has been trained on. It uses probabilities (what is the next most likely word in this sentence?) to create seemingly fluent text, but without any understanding of what it has created.

Second, as a consequence of the way it is trained, ChatGPT often makes factual errors and incorrect statements. When we asked it to create a biography for Julian Birkinshaw, it mentioned several books he wrote alongside others he did not write. The made-up book titles were plausible, but factually wrong. It also creates text with in-built biases, as a function of how it was trained. For example, it will often use the pronoun 'she' for nurses and 'he' for doctors because that's what its probability-based model comes up with. These biases are gradually being weeded out. There is also a lot of effort being put into guarding against illegal or immoral responses – though this work is fraught with difficulty because it's not obvious whose moral code ChatGPT's output should be screened against.

Third, ChatGPT is what techies call *narrow* AI – it is very good at one thing (creating text responses to prompts), but it cannot do anything else (for example, providing grief counselling or driving a car). We are still a very long way from a world of *general* AI, where the machine is multi-functional and operates at the level of a human. Our view is that it is unlikely we will see evidence of General AI in our lifetimes. But we could be wrong! The only thing we know for sure is that AI will continue to improve, and in sometimes unpredictable ways.

Put these points together and it should be clear that ChatGPT is a powerful but slightly dangerous tool. It appears to create insight and knowledge, but really it creates well-structured and fluent information that is based on but not fully tied to reality. Indeed, we can go further. ChatGPT creates what philosopher Harry Frankfurt calls 'bullshit' – words that are 'intended to persuade, without regard for the truth'.[6] There is already a huge amount of bullshit in today's post-truth society, with a range of actors – some real, some generated by bots – happily sharing their 'alternative facts' on social media, leading to a breakdown in trust and an increasingly polarized political culture. The explosive growth of social media is already changing our pacts of shared culture – democracy, civic life, networks of communications – in unpredictable and challenging ways. AI has the potential to exacerbate these problems further, threatening social cohesion.

INDIVIDUAL PRODUCTIVITY – HOW CAN I GET THE MOST OUT OF GENERATIVE AI?

User adoption of ChatGPT has been faster than any other product in history, reaching 1 million users in five days. Huge numbers of people are now using it in their daily working lives – a recent McKinsey study reported that 40 per cent of respondents were using Gen AI tools regularly.[7] So, most of the initial benefits of ChatGPT are at the individual level.

For example, soon after its launch, Julian needed to write a 1,000-word introduction to a business topic for his students. With a few careful prompts and a couple of iterations, about ten minutes' work, ChatGPT created a draft text. He edited this text, adding in a few ideas of his own, and the job was done and dusted in less than an hour. A year earlier, it would have taken four times as long. The same productivity boost is available in many professions, including marketing, advertising, law, consulting and software-writing.

Our advice to anyone involved in knowledge-work is simple – use ChatGPT to help you do your job. You bring experience, situational context and creative ideas; it provides the horsepower to synthesize existing information, structure an argument, review and critique your work, and offer points of view that you had not thought of. Think of it as a hardworking, know-it-all intern who has just joined your team. It doesn't understand your business at all, but delights in taking on the work that you don't have time for. And it doesn't even need to be thanked – although you may find it more helpful if you do!

Where have these productivity benefits been the greatest? The McKinsey study mentioned earlier suggests marketing and sales, product development and service operations are the places ChatGPT is used most – for example, in writing first drafts of documents, identifying trends and customer needs, and using chatbots (to talk to customers). It is also very good at writing computer code. But a couple of words of caution as well. First, make sure everyone understands the limitations of Generative AI, as noted above. There was a famous case in early 2023 where a lawyer cited legal precedents that had actually been invented by ChatGPT.[8] You need to check facts and rectify biases before using anything it comes up with. You also need to do some rewriting – most people can now spot ChatGPT-generated text quite easily and it's important that your text is written in your voice.

Second, remember that ChatGPT provides you with generic, lowest-common-denominator answers to your questions. In the words of Arka Dhar, a member of the product team at OpenAI, it 'excels at mediocrity',[9] which may be fine for those still getting up to speed, but it's not good enough for an ambitious individual or organization. ChatGPT has raised the bar for what a good-enough presentation or article looks like. The question you must answer is, how will I ensure that my output is way above that bar? What distinctive skills or insights will I bring to the table to make my work stand out? We will share some thoughts on what those distinctively human skills are later in the chapter.

BUSINESS PRODUCTIVITY – HOW CAN WE BECOME MORE EFFICIENT AND EFFECTIVE?

While the value of AI for individual productivity is now pretty obvious, the question of how AI is creating value at the level of the organization as a whole is more difficult to answer. In theory, the digital revolution (and here, we are talking about the last 30 years, not just the three years since ChatGPT was launched) should have resulted in dramatic improvements in business performance. Throughout the book, we have talked about how digital technology has enabled the creation of structures and systems that get work done in a hyper-efficient way, leading to lower production costs, fewer errors and less time spent by humans on repetitive tasks. But the data doesn't bear this out. It's a curious fact, but the aggregate statistics show a *declining* level of productivity growth in the major developed economies over the last 30 years. In the UK, for example, productivity growth has stalled completely since 2007.[10] The US Bureau of Labor Statistics says productivity growth in the US was 0.4 per cent per year 2005 to 2018. The UK was even worse, 0.1 per cent per year over same period.

Many explanations have been offered for this 'productivity puzzle'. Some observers note that it takes a long time for the benefits of IT investment to be realized. Others say our measures don't capture the benefits of new technology properly. For example, when you use a social networking app, the value you get from it counts for nothing in the statistics because you didn't pay for it.

Even taking these points into account, there is still a residual concern that digital technology isn't having its desired impact on business productivity. In our interpretation, this is because many established firms haven't made the needed changes in management techniques and structures to capture the potential benefits. One early study on this topic, for example, showed that productivity benefits from investing in new IT systems were only achieved by companies that adopted innovative working practices.[11]

Which brings us to the other important dimension of productivity, namely how to enable our colleagues to do their best work. And of course, AI (like other digital technologies before it) is something of a double-edged sword in this regard. It can be used as a tool for control or coercion. Consider the Amazon driver or call centre worker, whose every move – and every utterance – is scripted by an algorithm. Call centres are now sufficiently sophisticated that they can adapt the script in real time depending on the intonation and language used by the caller. Students of management will recognize this as a form of 'Neo-Taylorism', named after Frederick Winslow Taylor, the father of scientific management. His brutal attempts to optimize human effort by scripting a worker's every move were not that effective and were largely disavowed by the Human Relations movement that followed. But advances in AI now make it possible to put Taylor's ideas into practice to an extent he could not have imagined.

AI can also liberate us. It can be used to take on the tedious tasks that we don't want to do, enabling us to do the more interesting parts of our job better. Again, there are existing examples of how this might play out. Robotic Process Automation (RPA) is a basic form of AI that many companies are already deploying in such tasks as searching texts, correcting documents, invoice processing and so on. Nvidia's Jensen Huang sees the emergence of AI agents as a digital workforce, enhancing productivity and freeing up humans to focus on more value added work.

HOW TO USE GENERATIVE AI

So, what's the advice here? How should you use AI technology to improve your business productivity? It goes without saying that you need to learn how to use these new technologies, but there is still huge uncertainty about how quickly they will develop and what types of applications will be invented. So, it is useful to build on learning from earlier periods of technological change. We were fascinated by a conversation with John Behrens, the executive who led Pearson's work with IBM Watson, which we referenced at the beginning of this chapter (*see also* page 165). The key points from this interview are highlighted in the boxed text below (How will Generative AI play out? Lessons from Experience). In addition, we would make four specific points building on themes from earlier chapters.

First, **take a pragmatic fast-follower approach to AI investment**. It is tempting to seek some sort of first-mover advantage and in a few isolated cases that might work. But the risks of investing in the wrong technology, or getting in before it's ready for use, are huge. You should experiment in multiple, low-cost ways and keep an alert eye on how things are evolving, but making big early bets is unlikely to pay off.

It's important to stress that we're not saying that your company should be complacent about AI – that you should be resisting or downplaying the opportunity or the threat. Not at all. If you're behind on the learning curve of AI, you'll be behind on the experience curve, too. What we are saying, drawing on experience, is that incumbents should 'learn, don't guess'. Get ChatGPT and other tools into the hands of as many people across the company as possible as quickly as you can; encourage them to innovate and iterate; share what you learn widely and scale behind things that start to gain traction and validity. Just be careful that, for fear of missing out, you don't make big, expensive early bets on projects that may win you a gratifying headline short term but are unlikely longer term to be commercially successful.

Second, **invest in workplace and process redesign**. As noted earlier, research has shown how the productivity benefits of Information Technology accrue only to those firms that also rethink how they do their work. Or stated differently, if you try to optimize an out-dated process using technology, you end up frustrating your employees rather than enabling them.

A case in point is the world of professional services – for example, audit, law and consulting. For decades, their business model has relied on huge numbers of trainees working on tiresome entry-level jobs, an up-or-out system with professional exams and pyramid-shaped teams that allow senior people to earn a handsome return. Artificial Intelligence is now challenging this entire model. Earlier waves of technology killed off manufacturing jobs and data-processing jobs, now it's the turn of low-level professional jobs. The knock-on effects in terms of the size and staffing of teams, the skills required and indeed the profitability of these firms, will be sizeable. The firms that adapt their management structures most effectively – and re-engineer the training of their future talent – will be the winners.

An important principle in workplace redesign is to use AI as an enabling rather than a coercive force. As explained above, AI can be used in a coercive way (telling people what to do) or in an enabling way (helping them figure out what to do). And of course, when it's used to enable rather than coerce there are huge ancillary benefits in terms of worker morale and engagement. The point is that neither of these approaches is pre-determined. Your role as a leader is not to let the technology (or the company selling it) dictate the way forward. It is to formulate your own choice about the type of workplace you want for your workers and to deploy the latest technologies in a way that supports your objectives.

Third, remember that **it is at least as much about people as it is about technology**. A key lesson from previous waves of digital transformation is there is little value in applying new technology to outmoded systems and ways of working – and we're seeing the same trend play out with generative AI. A recent survey from the Upwork Research Institute found that while 96 per cent of C-suite leaders expect that AI will enhance productivity, 77 per cent of employees using AI say these tools have added to their workload and nearly half (47 per cent) of employees using AI report they do not know how to achieve the expected productivity gains.[12] This dichotomy is not to be unexpected in the early stages of the adoption of any new technology, but it won't be closed without concerted action. How can we redesign the organization to enhance its ability to apply AI in agile and iterative ways? How do we need to re-think ways of working and learn quickly from what employees are telling us about which AI tools help and which don't? How do we best invest in our people – through training and upskilling – so that they have the skills and the confidence to apply AI in productive and creative ways? Companies need to ensure they choose their AI applications wisely and are agile in how they use them.

Fourth, become **a responsible user of AI**. Learning the lessons from previous waves of technology adoption, many companies are being much more proactive much earlier in working through how they can use AI in a transparent, responsible and ethical manner. These approaches stress protecting data integrity and privacy, respecting intellectual property, enabling human interpretation and oversight, and valuing accuracy over hallucination. They are also likely to recognize that the massive data centres necessary to power AI are huge consumers of electricity and water. For example, the International Energy Agency estimates that global electricity demand from data centres will double in two years – equal to Japan's total annual energy consumption. Therefore, companies committed to net zero and related policies will have to work out how to take an environmentally sustainable approach to AI.

HOW WILL GENERATIVE AI PLAY OUT? LESSONS FROM EXPERIENCE

We discussed the transformative potential of Generative AI with John Behrens, the executive at Pearson who led its early work on Artificial Intelligence with IBM Watson. Here, we summarize his key insights, all of which echo important themes we have developed throughout the book.

Transformation, not just digitization. Generative AI will challenge the imagination of incumbent companies, as they seek to grasp the potential of Language Learning Models and the applications being built on them. It will take time for people to rethink what is possible and many will either ignore the new technology or use their prior mental model of the business and re-wrap it in a weak version of the new technology. By way of comparison, in the early days of the internet, the publishing industry moved to printing and distributing static text PDFs to check off the 'digital' requirement without realizing the real win wasn't in digital as a content type but rather in the creation and delivery of personalized, real-time interface through which it could offer its services (think Kindle versus PDF). John Behrens shared his view: '*As we go into the new AI world, we should be thinking about whether we are using it to repave the existing cow-path or to make new trails.*'

The challenge of new entrants is significant. The power of Generative AI is amazing, and what is even more amazing is how cheap its services are. Basic services are entirely free to individuals. Enterprise services, fully integrated into a firm's cloud infrastructure, cost around \$20–30 per month/user. For example, ChatGPT has integrated the running of computer software in python with its generation, thereby allowing these systems not only to generate ideas about actions, but also to start to implement those actions.

The point is that the barriers to entry, in terms of creating Generative AI based applications, are extremely low, making *'every college sophomore a potential competitor'*, as John Behrens warned us. To be sure, the investment required to create a new Large Language Model (LLM) are prohibitive, with only the big-tech players able to compete in that area, but as with any technology stack, it is the applications at the top that have the disruptive potential because they have the power to change consumer behaviour. Just as the mobile revolution enabled a whole set of new entrants (What's App, WeChat, TikTok), we can expect the Generative AI revolution to open opportunities for as-yet-unknown players.

Incumbents still have some big advantages. Even as new entrants emerge, we can expect established firms to respond quickly and with some success. This has been a key theme throughout the book and we expect it to retain its validity, even with all the current changes underway.

Consider IBM Watson again: being the world's leading educational publisher was a clear advantage for Pearson as its books provided a lot of text-based data (words) that could be used to train Watson. One of the downsides with ChatGPT is that if you ask a general question, you get a general/median answer and the possibility of hallucination. This risk is now being addressed by an approach called RAG – Retrieval Augmented Generation – where you give the system access to specific documents or a database and tell it to only give answers based on those documents and not to say anything that is not in the documents. For any incumbent with a huge amount of valuable, proprietary content, such as publishers, this is a major source of advantage – and explains why companies such as the *New York Times* are fighting hard to ensure that general LLMs are not being trained using their intellectual property.

Incumbents also have other big advantages. They have trusted brands, deep regulatory expertise, access to policymakers, distribution engines, large amounts of valuable, proprietary data.

They are well equipped to fight back against new entrants and to defend their market positions.

Detail matters – the application of Generative AI will vary by industry and domain. AI is what economists call a general-purpose technology, meaning that it can be used across multiple domains. However, that doesn't mean it can be used without careful customization. One important learning from Pearson's earlier work with Watson was the nature of linguistic variation across disciplines. For example, the type of words used in social sciences have a lot of overlap with words used in general colloquial language, which confused the Watson system and made it harder to train. In physical sciences, the vocabulary had dramatically less overlap so key words and phrases were more highly differentiated. As John Behrens observed: '*This is why you want linguists and psychologists on your teams, as well as data scientists; you are not trying to analyse data, you are trying to analyse the world.*'

The broader point here is that there is scope for specialists to emerge in every industry segment. For example, in the world of financial information provision, it is Refinitiv and Bloomberg that dominate, not Google, because Google has neither the dedicated expertise nor the market relationships that it would need to succeed there. This need for specialist expertise won't go away with Generative AI.

If you're not busy being born. Many of the biggest challenges in embracing Generative AI won't be technical but organizational and cultural. How self-aware an organization is in understanding itself, and its ability to embrace change and iterate continuously, will be crucial to its ability to deliver in an integrated design and delivery world. As John Behrens said: '*Thanks for pushing Pearson in the direction of innovation when we were all there; so many of the lessons we learned and ideas we adopted around change and digital transformation will be crucial in helping any organization's response to generative AI.*'

BUSINESS LEVEL CHOICES – WHAT IS OUR STRATEGY?

Everything we have said so far is about using AI (and digital technology more generally) within an existing business model or strategy. It answers the question, how can we serve our existing customers more efficiently and effectively? But strategy is about making choices, where to play and how to play. It's about beating the competition by coming up with something new that customers want to pay for. It's important to get this right, so we need to ask a different question: how will AI affect business strategy?

One obvious risk is that AI-based technologies will lead to greater convergence among competing firms. They are becoming more efficient. More of their activities are being outsourced and put on the Cloud. Interfaces between firms are becoming standardized. Online aggregators and retailers are encouraging price comparison. The net result of these trends is that executives are making more constrained decisions than in the past as they are operating within an established ecosystem. There is therefore pressure on them to take decisions that push them closer to their competitors. It's a low-risk, low-reward way of acting.

Our point is that these forces have always existed in business, but they are being amplified by the emergence of common IT infrastructure and by AI-enabled decision-making processes. Simply put, if the digital revolution has already pushed competitors to converge in how they **act** (how they make and distribute their products), the Gen AI revolution is now pushing competitors to converge in how they **think** (the ideas they come up with and develop). The net result is likely to be further reversion to the mean – towards lowest common denominator solutions that no one is excited about.

So, what's the role of the leader, the businessperson who is trying to do something innovative and distinctive? It boils down to doing the things AI cannot do – taking a more 'human' approach to strategy that plays on such qualities as creativity, intuition and empathy. In terms of what this looks like in practice, here are some specific pieces of advice. Again, we believe that incumbents can draw heavily from what we've learnt about leading through previous waves of digital disruption to guide them through the new era of AI.

Harness your disruptive mindset

A rational, tech-driven calculus would favour putting investment in those areas where the payoff is most direct, but in many AI-related cases, that's not yet clear. For example, a huge amount is being invested by Big Tech to build the infrastructure to support AI – buying land, constructing new data centres, buying the hardware, including the specialized clusters of chips needed to train and run large language learning models – but investors are unclear as yet what all the business models and payoffs are. The most successful strategies are likely to be the ones that acknowledge the inherent uncertainty in the future. As Jeremy Darroch, former CEO of Sky, told us in a wider context:

> One of the biggest mistakes executives and businesses can make is wanting to predict the future in an overly precise way. We're here today and we will be X in a few years' time. Sometimes, the pressure of being a senior executive is almost wanting to be able to answer that question, to be the expert in that. Of course, when you think about it, that is crazy. How can you predict where the world is going to be? What we started to think about was this idea of shifting plates and big thematics that we could see with some confidence, placing our bets there.

The best way forward, in other words, is to make calculated bets based on a good understanding of trends but with some level of courage as well and accepting that you may be wrong. Every famous innovation story, from Ikea to the iPhone to Tesla, was a huge bet on something that wasn't entirely obvious at the time and required a lot of upfront investment.

Successful firms, in other words, take resources away from their short-term best use in order to give themselves the chance to create even more value over the long term. This 'one step back, two steps forward' logic manifests itself in many ways – risky R&D projects, pursuing sustainability goals, paying above-market wages to improve loyalty, and so on. We actually take it for granted that firms will do many of these things, but our argument is that they involve judgements that AI is ill-equipped to help us with. AI can devise seemingly cunning strategies that look prescient (recall the famous case of AlphaGo, an AI that beat top Go player Lee Sedol in 2016[13]), but only when the rules of the game are pre-determined and stable.

It's not easy to provide specific advice on how to do this, but the starting point is an innovative or disruptive frame of mind, or what Amazon's Jeff Bezos calls a 'willingness to be misunderstood'.

Retain your identity and focus on purpose

There is a second dimension to long-term thinking and that is its impact on individual and team motivation. Purpose is a 'moral or spiritual call to action' that leads people to put in discretionary effort – to work long hours and to bring their passion and creativity to the workplace.

This notion that a firm has a social quality, a purpose or identity, is well established. But it still arouses suspicion among those who believe that people are motivated largely through extrinsic rewards. Our view is that you just need to look at charities, open-source software movements and many other not-for-profit organizations to realize that many people work harder when money is not involved. And it is the capacity of a leader to articulate a sense of purpose, in a way that creates emotional resonance with followers, that is uniquely human.

Successful firms, in other words, develop a sense of identity and purpose that attracts employees and customers. For example, even though firms are experimenting with blockchain technology to build a system that cannot be hacked or misused by a few opportunists, its limited uptake at the current time suggests people still prefer to put their faith in other people. This is why another lesson to apply to the AI challenge is to use it to renew your company's sense of purpose – and your identity. What is it you do that is of enduring value to your customers which won't be changed by AI and could in fact be enhanced by it? For example, the fuel that fires AI is data. As a leader in your industry how you can use AI to unlock the insights and innovation lying as yet unrealized in all your proprietary data – all you know about your customers and your industry? For example, the biggest challenge facing big pharma is the productivity of R&D – it costs billions, it takes decades and 90 per cent of it doesn't work. According to Emma Walmsley, CEO of GSK, applying AI to research *'is the holy grail for us. That is where we can create real material value.'*[14]

Nurture unreasonable behaviour
Another lesson we can apply from previous waves of digital transformation is that incumbents are likely to need less hierarchy and more adhocracy if they are to rise to the challenge. There are many famous cases of mavericks who succeeded by challenging the rules, such as Steve Jobs or Richard Branson. In the words of George Bernard Shaw, we think of these people as unreasonable – they seek to adapt the world to their view, rather than learn to fit in. And if we want to see firms move beyond what is already known and proven – to create new market opportunities – more of these types of people would be useful.

Unreasonableness is antithetical to the world of AI. Computers work either through sophisticated algorithms or by inference from prior data, and in both cases the capacity to make an entirely out-of-the-box leap doesn't exist. The widespread adoption of co-pilots – integrated into Microsoft teams and other workforce tools – can make companies more susceptible to groupthink, making it harder to hear the contrarian voice that, as we've seen so often throughout this book, is vital for leaders to seek out and listen to. For example, in the world of investment management, robo advisors are not just making trades, they are also providing investment advice to investors – and at a fraction of the cost of human financial advisors. But as the *Financial Times*[15] said a few years back, 'When it comes to investing, human stupidity beats AI.' In other words, if you want to beat the market, you need to be a contrarian – you need to make investments that go against the perceived wisdom at the time and you need to accept the risk that your judgement or your timing might be wrong. These qualities are – at the moment – distinctively human.

In sum, one of the distinctive qualities of successful firms is their unreasonable behaviour. Of course, many do their best to drive out variance, by using tight control systems and punishing failure. As AI becomes more influential, through the automation of basic activities and simple contracts, it becomes even more important for firms to push in the other direction – to nurture unorthodox thinking, encourage experimentation and tolerate failure. This requires more adhocracy and less bureaucracy.

Understand where your company sits in the wider AI ecosystem
Just as over the last decade companies have had to work out their platform strategy – whether they aspire to be a platform in their own right or, more likely, are deploying a range of strategies to position themselves as part of a wider ecosystem dependent on one or more of the major technology platforms – so they now need to do the same in the world of generative AI. It seems likely that AI will cement the power of Big Tech and the relatively small number of startups (such as OpenAI) that are tightly aligned with them. As things stand today, it is only a small number of very big technology companies who can afford to build and maintain the vast data centres – with their tens or even hundreds of thousands of GPUs – necessary to power the large language learning models vital to enable generative AI. Can you survive and prosper by deploying AI models that are available to you through your Cloud provider? For example, Microsoft Azure claims to have 1,600 AI models available to its users to deploy. Are you primarily looking to deploy those tools to improve the efficiency of your back office and how you run your business? Or is your primary focus on deploying AI to offer enhanced personalized and customized services to your customers? If so, to what extent will that require you to create your own bespoke AI tools? As a company, do you own a large amount of proprietary data that can be applied to help your customers solve specific problems precisely and accurately? If so, you may be best focusing on domain specific, narrower focused language learning models, which may be more affordable, stable, easily updatable and with significantly fewer risks of hallucination. As

we are still in the very early stages of the generative AI revolution, the answers are unlikely to be clear-cut, but they are the sort of questions that companies need to be asking themselves.

This means in turn a battle with prioritization: should you continue with the modernization of your technology platform – as we described in Chapter 5, *see also* page 109 – or should you shift engineering resources into generative AI? Everyone will decide differently, dependent in part on how they see generative AI changing their business. However, as with previous waves of digital transformation, as Amazon's Andy Jassy and other technology leaders have pointed out, unless your enabling technology – your foundational infrastructure – is right, you will find it very hard to be successful with generative AI. For example, using AI to unleash value in your proprietary data requires a good data strategy and supporting platform already in place.

Be proactive in telling your story

As with grandiose claims made for previous waves of technology, messianic quotes about how AI will transform our world – how this could be a turning point in human history – will excite some people and scare many more. And these emotions will be heightened when a company starts to deploy AI within its business. It has the potential to be both discombobulating and disempowering. So, learning again from previous waves of digital transformation, senior leadership need to combine the light on the hill – the compelling vision as to how AI can help the company serve its customers better – with a very immediate, pragmatic plan for implementation. In the earlier stages, you may want to encourage teams to try lots of different AI tools and be nimble enough to scale those that add value and switch off quickly those that don't prove helpful.

Externally, too, in engaging with shareholders, we can apply the lessons discussed in the previous chapter. Your shareholders want to know that you're alive to the opportunities and the threats, that you have a vision and a plan, are open-minded regarding the challenges and able to articulate the strengths of your business that will be sustained – and even enhanced – by the widespread adoption of generative AI.

AI probably has the potential to be most disruptive most quickly to those digital content-rich industries – in areas like information, publishing, arts and entertainment – whose intellectual property is delivered by bit and byte. It's no surprise that these are the industries that are both among the quickest to adopt AI within their own businesses and, learning the lessons from past battles, also the most assertive in seeking to protect their intellectual property. *The New York Times* has taken legal action to prevent copyright infringement of content related to AI systems,[16] while the *Wall Street Journal* and *The Times* newspaper owner, News Corp, has reached a commercial agreement with OpenAI, giving it permission to use some of its content in response to user questions. For most other industries, the impact of AI is likely to play out over a longer time period and, at least for some time yet, have a less dramatic effect.

We expect that, with AI as with previous waves of technology, incumbents will find ways to adapt and ultimately to prosper – as they apply all that they've learnt from past disruptions and transformations.

SOCIETAL IMPACT – THE FUTURE OF WORK AND OF SOCIETY

More than any other technology breakthrough of the digital age, AI appears to strike at the heart of our intelligence and creativity, of what makes us human. The qualities that until now we alone have possessed now seem capable of being replicated – or at least mimicked – by a machine. The opening lines of Charles Dickens' novel, *A Tale of Two Cities* – 'It was the best of times, it was the worst of times' – capture just how epoch-making he saw the events of the French Revolution, but it seems positively understated compared to the way some Generative AI champions see the opportunities and the threats that the AI revolution could bring. Here, for example, is Sam Altman, founder of OpenAI:

The best case is so unbelievably good, it is hard for me to imagine... The bad case is like lights out for all of us.[17]

And yet, as we noted earlier, this mythical, all-powerful AGI that's going to take over our world and determine our future with its superhuman skills is to our mind still only vaguely defined, with no credible predictions for it happening any time soon.

AI, like all previous waves of technology, is a tool made by humans and which should be deployed by our companies to serve our customers and gain competitive advantage; and for wider economic, intellectual and social benefit. It is true that it is *potentially* the most powerful technological tool yet created – and it is a big worry that its development is currently largely controlled by just seven very big technology companies and a relatively small number of startups, often funded by the very same companies. So, it is important that the wider business community – including the leaders of large incumbent companies – are actively involved in the debate about how AI will affect jobs, careers, education and society more widely, and the choices we make as a result.

Throughout history – going right back to the Luddites in the early stages of the Industrial Revolution – it has always been easier for people to see the existing jobs that will be destroyed by new technology than imagine the new ones that will be created. We can see that again today. PwC warns that a third of all jobs globally could be automated by the mid-2030s;[18] Goldman Sachs report that the equivalent of 300 million jobs could be automated away.[19] It is likely that many clerical and professional jobs, in particular, are at risk through AI. And yet, we know from previous waves of technology that, over time, technology tends to create more new jobs – because it opens up new fields of activity – than it destroys. This is the famous process of 'creative destruction' sketched out originally by political economist Joseph Schumpeter. An article in the *Wall Street Journal* showed the dramatic reduction in numbers of bookkeepers, audit clerks and accountants from 1988 to today, following the mass adoption of spreadsheet technology (VisiCalc, Lotus 123 and MS Excel).[20] This reduction was matched by the dramatic growth in analyst and financial manager roles, as the application of spreadsheets to business challenges skyrocketed. There was also a significant growth in the number of accountants and auditors, to provide oversight of this boom in analytical work.

Will the past be a reliable guide to our AI future? That is largely our choice to make and if we deploy AI as we should – as a complement and not a substitute to human thought and creativity, as a means of enhancing our productivity – then that should hold true this time, too.

Most jobs are made up of a multitude of different tasks, some of which will become obsolete while others won't. Any job can be broken down into the knowledge, skills and abilities required to perform it and the specific tasks and activities it requires (the US Department of Labor's O*Net survey defines every occupation in the US economy in these terms). Technology tends to automate some of these tasks – and acquire some of the knowledge and skills – but never all of them. So, over time, the nature of work changes and hybrid roles emerge. As AI tools are embedded into the workflows of most companies, this trend is likely to exacerbate.

We've talked in previous chapters about the challenge for incumbent companies in closing the gap between the exponential rate of technological change and the more linear way in which humans adapt to it. The speed with which AI is being developed and adopted means that existing jobs are being disrupted and new, hybrid roles are emerging at ever greater speed, making it all the more important that companies and individuals are constantly re-skilling and upskilling to keep pace with these emerging technologies.

We have already discussed the need for workplace redesign in business, but the challenge is much wider than that because we will need to rethink whole categories of jobs across the public and private sectors, including the training provided and the qualifications people gain to do them.

Which jobs are most at risk now? Clearly those involving simple analytical or text-based work are under threat – transcription, translation, copy-editing, searches of legal documents, basic writing tasks, to name just a few. Many call centre and customer service roles will also be lost to chatbots, though we all know (from experience) that a human touch will still be vital for some elements of customer service. Indeed, many companies are using AI tools to help call centre employees deliver a better service rather than simply displacing them. The number of repetitive manual jobs – for example, cleaners and checkout assistants – will continue to fall as automation becomes smarter.

Equally, there are many jobs likely to be unaffected by AI. Many people would argue that high-end knowledge workers, from CEOs to lawyers to engineers, are paid to exercise judgement and to get things done through influence and persuasion – innately human qualities that should prove robot-proof. Indeed, the way in which the relative earnings power of these professions has grown significantly in the last 20 years is often attributed to an 'expertise bottleneck': that, in our increasingly complex world, there is always demand for more expertise. David Autor, of Massachusetts Institute of Technology, argues that thoughtful use of AI could enable people with less experience and training to make some of these professional judgements, easing the bottleneck of expertise. This in turn would help to rebuild the American middle class 'hollowed out' by technology over the last 20 years, making things like legal or financial advice or healthcare more affordable:

> *AI's capacity to weave information and rules with acquired experience to support decision-making can be applied to enable a larger set of workers possessing complementary knowledge to perform some of the higher-stakes decision-making tasks that are currently arrogated to elite experts, e.g., medical care to doctors, document production to lawyers, software coding to computer engineers, and undergraduate education to professors. My thesis is not a forecast but an argument about what is possible: AI, if used well, can assist with restoring the middle-skill, middle-class heart of the US labor market that has been hollowed out by automation and globalization.*[21]

Note the caution: *not a forecast but an argument about what is possible.* AI's impact on society will, in large part, be determined by the choices we make, what we believe is possible and act to make happen. There are many socially vital but often poorly paid jobs – for example, nursing and care work – where emotional intelligence and empathy combined with specialist knowledge and skills are central to the work and which seem destined to remain in the hands of human workers. These roles, too, are likely to change over time. As more people live longer, the costs of residential care for the elderly are growing rapidly, creating a major challenge for many developed economies, in particular. Spiralling costs and growing demand require societies to continue to find more effective ways to care for more elderly people in their own homes rather than in a residential institution. This care can be enhanced significantly by breakthroughs in wearable technology and AI, making it both much more effective and affordable. This in turn will require nursing and care staff to acquire new skills to be able to use these tools in pre-emptive ways, potentially to the mutual benefit of society and themselves – if these new higher-skilled, hybrid roles attract higher salaries – funded by savings in expensive remedial and residential care.

This is just one small example to illustrate the point that AI does not exist in isolation – there are a whole series of other trends (demographic, environmental, geopolitical) that will shape its adoption and development. AI is not some mythical superpower handed down by an all-powerful digital god and controlled by a small number of Silicon Valley deities. AI applications are products created by humans and we can decide what powers we want the software to have, how we chose to use it and what value we attribute to the new services that follow from them.

AI is better at finding patterns in complex datasets and generating content quickly. People are much better at creativity, intuition, relationship-building, judgement and empathy. That means we are better at writing, at planning and developing new ideas, at reading body language, at comforting the upset and sick, at applying common sense in complex or stressful situations and at leading people through times of change. As individuals and as companies, we should cherish and burnish these distinctly human qualities – always important capabilities, but with the AI revolution now underway, more vital than ever.

WHAT ARE THE IMPLICATIONS FOR GOVERNMENT AND SOCIETY?

First, there is a need for new regulation. Like any new technology, Generative AI creates huge worries for regulators because they don't have a framework for defining the necessary guardrails around its use. The Italian data regulator briefly banned ChatGPT, before changing its mind. US and EU regulatory agencies (at the time of writing) are now looking into various issues – for example, whether ChatGPT infringed data protection or IP rules in building its model, and how to ensure its output doesn't stray into illegal and dangerous territory. We can expect some significant new regulations over the next couple of years, and indeed this has been welcomed by many players, including Sam Altman, the OpenAI founder. But it will be messy – we know from previous generations of new technologies that agile tech firms are good at finessing and sidestepping the efforts of regulators who try to rein in their activities.

Second, our education systems need upgrading and rethinking. As touched on earlier, anyone can now produce lowest-common-denominator output with almost no knowledge of what they are doing, so we need to come up with new ways of educating people on frameworks and concepts and how to apply them. Of course, we have been here before – the pocket calculator made slide rules obsolete and mental arithmetic less important, so the way maths was taught and assessed adapted accordingly. Students will need to learn how to harness AI effectively, as well as how to be more creative, intuitive and empathetic. How, for example, do we redefine Higher Education, seamlessly integrating AI into teaching and research? That long-held vision – of technology enabled, personalized, lifelong learning – seems more achievable than ever before. But it can only be achieved if, as Jeremy Kahn[22] puts it, universities see AI as a copilot not an autopilot, designed in a way that is truly collaborative with human engagement at multiple stages. As in every other sphere, AI in Higher Education must enhance, not displace human intelligence – enough AI to make students more productive, not so much that they lose the essential cognitive skills and abilities that we described earlier. There will need to be a greater focus on experiential learning and inter-disciplinary approaches, recognizing that the increasingly hybrid nature of many roles combine elements of both the sciences and the humanities. Joseph Aoun, President of Northeastern University (and a colleague of John Fallon), advocates a 'humanics' model,[23] covering data literacy, to manage the flow of big data; technological literacy, to understand how AI actually works; and human literacy, encompass-ing the humanities, communication and design.

Third, creative destruction (new jobs emerging after old jobs are killed off) never happens without some pain – the people who lose their jobs aren't necessarily able to build the skills to do the new jobs. Some of the new jobs will be in the wrong places and at lower salary levels, and some companies will go bust. Again, we have been here many times before. Government has a vital role to play in helping individuals and communities through these difficult transitions and large incumbent companies also have an important role to play. For example, they can deploy AI applications as career coaches, helping employees to plan a personalized career path which anticipates how technology may change or disrupt their current role and how they can burnish existing knowledge and skills – and acquire new ones – to the mutual benefit of them personally and their employer.

One of the most striking features of the last 30 years is how tech-nology and related developments have lifted hundreds of millions in the developing world out of absolute poverty while many in the developed world have suffered greater relative income inequality. This latter trend has caused wider social and political stress, espe-cially in Europe and North America. As a society, how can we deploy AI to sustain the progress we've seen in the developing world, while reversing the income inequality trend we see in the world's richest economies, so that all parents can once again expect their children to have a better quality of life than their own? No easy remedies exist here, but clearly governments of all persuasions know they must find ways of balancing the gains from technology and redistributing wealth more equitably in order to keep society together. AI, like all forms of technology, is not some mystical life force but something that has been created by humans and we do have choices as to how we deploy it. What steps would a company and a society take if it chose to take the optimistic view – and tried, for example, to make David Autor's thesis of what's possible a reality?

CONCLUSIONS

Many observers have argued that the Generative AI revolution puts us at a unique point in human history. In *Homo Deus: A Brief History of Tomorrow*, bestselling Israeli author Yuval Noah Harari calls it *the great decoupling*, where for the first time in human evolution there is a possible schism between consciousness (subjective awareness) and intelligence (problem solving). This decoupling, he argues, creates huge risks for society in terms of inequality and a loss of social cohesion.[24]

Our point in this chapter – and indeed throughout the whole book – has been to underline that leaders have the agency and the responsibility to prevent this happening within their own organizations. Their job is to *actively recouple* consciousness and intelligence, to ensure there is a human quality to their products and services, and to safeguard the features of work that make it worth doing.

We might like to pretend this is a new argument, but it's not. In his 1982 book, *Megatrends*, futurist John Naisbitt coined the term high tech/high touch, arguing that it is incumbent on us to '*balance the material wonders of technology with the spiritual demands of our human race*'.[25] Since he made this observation in the early years of the computer revolution, Naisbitt could not have foreseen at the time just how advanced digital technology would become but the fundamental leadership challenge he identified remains the same.

Back in 1982, getting the high-tech/high-touch balance wasn't easy. With AI, it is getting a lot harder. As a result, it is a good time to remember that leadership requires attention to both behaviour and character. The best leaders aren't just good at inspiring others to achieve a challenging goal, they are also clear about what they stand for as individuals. In other words, human integrity around what is right and wrong has always mattered enormously, but it will matter even more as the world becomes increasingly influenced by AI.

AFTERWORD

We wrote this book as an equal partnership and indeed the process of writing helped each of us gain a more rounded perspective on the challenges of digital transformation and the opportunities for incumbents to be resurgent in the face of change. And we thank Adam Bouzelmate also for his excellent contributions throughout. But one important difference in our experience base is that while Julian has observed and participated in a number of digital trans-formations, John has actually *lived* it, as the former CEO of a major global company going through a major industry disruption. This short final chapter is his own personal reflection on what he learnt from his time at the top.

The Big Bets conference we talked about in the introduction to this book was facilitated by Alan Murray, long-time executive editor of Fortune business magazine. Before retiring from Fortune last summer to start a new venture, Alan wrote a daily email – the CEO Daily – in which he chronicled the challenges faced by the leaders of large incumbent companies in managing their way through digital transformation. In one of his emails,[1] he tells the story of hosting a dinner for a group of senior CFO's with Andrew McAfee, digital innovation guru at the MIT Sloan School. McAfee asks his audience:

> When you look at the head-to-head battles between the upstart companies and the incumbents of the industrial era, in how many of those battles has the incumbent won or even held steady?

Murray pushes back, arguing that, in his view, many incumbents have done far better against digital upstarts than anyone expected a decade ago. McAfee dismisses the challenge:

Continuing to exist is a really low bar.

That feels like a low blow. Industrial incumbents are doing much more than continuing to exist, as Julian's data on the relative stability in the make-up of the Fortune 500 over the last 40 years – with which we started the book – shows. Of course, they're not competing head-to-head with the extraordinarily wealthy Big Tech companies, who invested $106 billion in AI in just the first six months of 2024, but they are proving effective in seeing off the disruptive threat of so-called Little Tech. Far more unicorns have turned into unicorpses than incumbents have gone the way of Kodak. Incumbents of the industrial era are growing, and they are resurgent.

A regular refrain of the CEO Daily emails is how any conversation about technology very quickly develops into a conversation about people. It was true that day in Brooklyn when my fellow CEOs complained of being 'bruised from head to toe' from trying to change the culture of their organizations. And it was also true of every day of my eight years as Pearson CEO. How do I lead through change? How do I get teams to embrace rather than resist company transformation? In the very first in-house speech I gave as CEO, I quoted the economist, John Maynard Keynes, writing some 60 years earlier:

> The idea of the future being different from the present is so repugnant to our conventional modes of thought and behaviour that we, most of us, offer great resistance to acting it out in practice.[2]

The confidence I expressed that day – that my Pearson colleagues would, at least on this specific point, prove the late, great John Maynard Keynes wrong – would ultimately prove to be justified, but it was far harder and took much longer to get there than I could ever have known.

In Chapter 1, we distinguished between digital transformation and disruption. Every large established organization needs a transformation, to refashion and remake themselves for the digital age. A smaller number of large incumbents – mostly in media and related industries – face something far more disruptive: a technology enabled breakthrough that fundamentally upends their business and threatens their very existence.

Leading through such a disruption is, in many ways, a contact sport. As you create new things, the old things get bruised, battered, broken, bent out of shape. It is a very human process and so I think it is important for leaders – especially in the era of AI – to focus on the things that make us uniquely human because, as we've stressed repeatedly, digital transformation is at least as much about the people as it is about the technology.

You need a wider sense of purpose. *Throughout my 23 years at Pearson, the company championed proudly the mantra that 'profits sustain us but don't define us. What defines us is doing something important to society and doing it well.' When our main means of making money was badly disrupted, we learnt that the sustaining bit is actually very important. Purposeful companies without profit don't survive for long. If the profits are under pressure, then so are you. But when that happens, the defining part becomes more important too. And I believe that an important reason why Pearson is emerging resurgent, and as a stronger, faster-growing business, is that the disruption tested our sense of purpose – our belief that we had a vital role to play in helping people progress in their lives through learning – and strengthened it.*

You need to stand in the shoes of others. *I probably bored colleagues in the company with how often I quoted a scene from Harper Lee's book* To Kill a Mockingbird *when the character, Scout Finch, quotes her father – Atticus – as saying that you never really know somebody until you stand in their shoes and walk around in them. This quality is always important; it is vital in times of hard, difficult change. You can't lead a company through digital transformation unless you take the time to really understand what the people in it – and those dependent on it – think and feel.*

You need reserves of resilience, which you draw on at some times and replenish at others. *In my experience, colleagues can be unbelievably resilient in very trying times and over a long period of time – and then suddenly find life very difficult often because of something that seems relatively trivial. It's not their fault, they've not done anything wrong – it's simply that we pushed them too hard for too long and exhausted their reserves of resilience. You need to give them the time and space to replenish those reserves – or preferably give them the chance to do that when their tank of resilience is still at least a quarter full.*

Resilience, in part, comes from perspective. *There were times at Pearson when I'd wish somebody would compliment me on something other than my perceived resilience, but if I did seem able to absorb extreme pressure and deal with extended periods of bad news, I think it was that I always tried to retain a sense of perspective. When I was treated for cancer – three years before I was appointed CEO – it used to drive me mad when friends or colleagues would say something like: 'you'll be alright, John, because you're a fighter.' As well-meaning as it was, the comment provoked a feeling in me that, somehow, if I wasn't alright, it would be my fault that I hadn't fought hard enough. When, as anyone who has ever been in a similar position will know, cancer is something that in many ways you endure, rather than fight; and through your treatment, you learn to distinguish between the things that are in your control and the many things that aren't. This perspective helped me at Pearson. I learnt not to rail about the things I couldn't control – such as declining college enrolments, or the 20 years of rampant textbook price inflation that had created the second-hand market that was now proving so damaging, or the oodles of venture capital cash pouring into startups without credible business plans. Instead, I chose to focus on the things we could control – the new digital services that enabled better learning outcomes, at more affordable prices; the efficiency savings and technology investment that made that possible.*

You need to work hard. *This may seem a somewhat old-fashioned view – and I don't for a minute deride the greater emphasis these days on work/life balance and ensuring that employees look after their mental and physical health. We made progress on both fronts in my time as CEO, but the reality is you're not going to survive and prosper through a time of disruption unless you're willing to work hard – sometimes very hard, and often for extended periods of time.*

You must learn how to 'pass it on'. *The leadership role is often situational; you don't get to choose the wider industry context in which you operate. Sometimes, the task chooses you. For example, I didn't set out to go down in Pearson's corporate history as the CEO who sold great British media icons like the* Financial Times *and* Penguin, *or who reduced costs radically, with thousands of jobs lost as a result (although many new jobs were created, too.) But that's what was required to ensure the company's survival and independence.*

An important point to note in Pearson's story is that while managing a decade of analogue decline in College textbook sales, we invested in growing adjacent and largely digital businesses – in assessment & certification, virtual learning, language learning, workforce skills, courseware. The market capitalization of Pearson would only start to grow again when the profits generated by these growing digital businesses – as they scaled – outstripped the profits lost from the declining analogue sales. I realized that this tipping point was only going to happen beyond my tenure as CEO and that I would not be in situ to see many of the benefits of all the hard work we'd done materialize. But like the teacher in the play, The History Boys, *by Alan Bennett,[3] I realized that sometimes the best thing you can do is to take the parcel and 'pass it on', not for you but for the benefit of others. That's the game I committed to play. I resolved that nothing was going to stop me from always trying to make the right decision for the long-term future of the business – and to 'pass it on' in the very best possible shape I could.*

And you must be always beating on. *Over 20 years ago, in one of the last columns he wrote before his untimely death, the* Financial Times *journalist, Peter Martin, quoted F. Scott Fitzgerald, chronicler of the dynamic age of modern finance (and who has already made one appearance in this book). It was Fitzgerald, Peter wrote, who in the closing words of* The Great Gatsby, *best captured the way in which the capitalist economy pushes individuals and businesses forward against natural human inertia:*

> 'So, we beat on, boats against the current, borne back ceaselessly into the past.'

Peter's point was that fundamental to the success of all great companies is the belief that action today, despite the cost and inconvenience and uncertainty that change always brings, will be rewarded tomorrow. Great companies never lose faith in their essential magic, their impulse forward, their push against the tide.

It is the people *of these companies that beat on – through all the pain and chaos, the hopes and dreams that disruption brings; all the challenges and frustrations, the excitement and opportunities of large-scale transformation – to secure a resurgent future.*

They'll go on doing so for many years to come.

NOTES AND REFERENCES

INTRODUCTION

1   Birkinshaw, J. (2022). 'How incumbents survive and thrive', *Harvard Business Review*, *100*(1–2), 36–42.

2   Hinssen, P. (2020). *The Phoenix and the Unicorn*. Newton Engineering. Gerstner Jr, L. V. (2009). *Who says elephants can't dance?: Leading a great enterprise through dramatic change*. Zondervan.

3   Markides, C.C. & Geroski, P.A. (2004). *Fast Second: How Smart Companies Bypass Radical Innovation to Enter and Dominate New Markets*. John Wiley & Sons.

4   Many variants of this quotation exist. The original is from F. Scott Fitzgerald's book *The Crack-Up*, published in 1945.

CHAPTER 1

1   Jack, A. (2019). 'Pearson accelerates push to digital-first publishing', *Financial Times*, 16 July 2019.

2   Phare, C. (2019). 'The death of textbooks?' MSU Denver RED. red .msudenver.edu. 6 September 2019.

3   Wan, T. (2019). 'Pearson Signals Major Shift From Print by Making All Textbook Updates "Digital First", EdSurge News. 15 July. www.edsurge .com.

4   Tuttle, D. (2010). 'Avoiding "America's Biggest Rip-offs"', *TIME Magazine*, 4 February 2010. Business.time.com

5   One other point to note in Pearson's story is that while managing a decade of decline in College Publishing, we invested in growing adjacent businesses – in assessment & certification, virtual learning, English language learning, workforce skills – on the back of our incumbency. The market valuation of Pearson started to grow again as soon as the profit growth from these adjacent businesses – as they scaled – was higher than the profit loss from declining college textbook sales. In these adjacent businesses, digital presented the opportunity

to grow incrementally whereas in College publishing, you were losing high-price print sales to a combination of the secondary market and lower-price digital substitutes.

6   Christensen, C. (1996). 'The Innovator's Dilemma', Cambridge, MA: Harvard Business Press.

7   Christensen, C. (1996) op cit.

8   This case study of Sandvik is taken from: Visnjic, I., Birkinshaw, J. & Linz, C. (2022). 'When gradual change beats radical transformation', *MIT Sloan Management Review*, 63(3), 74–8.

9   Markides, C. & Charitou, C.D. (2004). 'Competing with dual business models: A contingency approach', *Academy of Management Perspectives*, 18(3), pp.22–36.

10 Burgelman, R.A. & Grove, A.S. (1996). 'Strategic dissonance', *California Management Review*, 38(2), 8–28.

11 Goddard, J., Birkinshaw, J. & Eccles, T. (2012). 'Uncommon sense: how to turn distinctive beliefs into action', *MIT Sloan Management Review*.

CHAPTER 2

1   McKinsey (2020). 'Building a digital New York Times: CEO Mark Thompson', 10 August 2020.

2   Anderson, P. & Tushman, M.L. (1990). 'Technological Discontinuities and Dominant Designs: A Cyclical Model of Technological Change', *Administrative Science Quarterly*, 35, 604–33.

3   Linden, Alexander & Fenn, Jackie (2003). 'Understanding Gartner's hype cycles', Gartner.

4   Birkinshaw, J. (2023). 'How Incumbent Firms Respond to Emerging Technologies: Comparing Supply-Side and Demand-Side Effects', *California Management Review*, 66(1).

5   Markides, C. & Geroski, P. (2005). 'Fast second: how smart companies bypass radical innovation to enter and dominate new markets', San Francisco, Ca: Jossey-Bass.

6   Hamel, Gary (1999). 'Bringing Silicon Valley Inside', *Harvard Business Review*, 77(5): 71–7.

7   Bambrough, Billy (2020). 'JPMorgan—Bitcoin's "Biggest Enemy"—Suddenly Appears to Be Going All in on Crypto', *Forbes*, 2 June 2024.

8 Kestenbaum, Richard (2024). 'Unilever's Sale of Dollar Shave Club Feels like a Celebrity Divorce', *Forbes*, 20 June 2024.

9 Lunden, Ingrid (2023). 'The Fall of Babylon: Failed Telehealth Startup Once Valued at $2B Goes Bankrupt, Sold for Parts. TechCrunch', 31 August 2023.

10 Here is one free-access story about WeWork's demise: Zeitlin, Matthew (2019). 'Why WeWork went wrong', *Guardian*, 20 December 2019.

CHAPTER 3

1 Chan Kim, W. & Mauborgne, Renée (2005). *Blue Ocean Strategy*, Boston, Mass.: Harvard Business School Press.

2 Drucker, Peter F. (1974). *Management: Tasks, Responsibilities, Practises*, New York: Harper Business.

3 *Financial Times*. (2022). 'Mercedes and BMW Offload Car-Sharing Venture to Stellantis', 3 May 2022.

CHAPTER 4

1 For example: Egelhoff, W.G. (1982). 'Strategy and structure in multinational corporations: An information-processing approach', *Administrative Science Quarterly*, 435–58.

2 Kotter, J. (2012). 'Change Fatigue: Taking Its Toll on Your Employees?' *Forbes*, 8 February 2012.

3 Ferguson, Niall (2017). *The Square and the Tower: Networks, Hierarchies and the Struggle for Global Power*, London: Allen Lane.

4 This quote was taken from a blog site 'Bob MacDonald on Business' in 2012. However, it seems this site has now been taken down. It's a nice quote, and we are happy to acknowledge Bob MacDonald as its author.

5 Hamel, Gary & Michele Zanini (2020). *Humanocracy: Creating Organizations as Amazing as the People inside Them*, Boston, Mass: Harvard Business Review Press.

6 Birkinshaw, J. & Ridderstråle, J. (2020). *Fast/forward: Make Your Company Fit for the Future*, Stanford University Press.

7 Kniberg, Henrik (2014). 'Spotify Engineering Culture (Part 1)', Spotify Engineering, 27 March 2014.

8 Birkinshaw, Julian, Mark, Ken & Chevrollier, Nicolas (2019) 'ENGIE's GEM Business Unit: Towards a New Way of Working', London Business School teaching case. www.publishing.london.edu.

9   Gill, Lisa (2024). 'Reinventing Big Pharma: Bayer's Shift towards Dynamic Shared Ownership', *Medium*. 20 February 2024. https://reimaginaire.medium.com.

10   There is also another meaning of the word 'culture', which is the notion of national culture. In other words, the set of values and beliefs that we almost inherited as we grow up in a particular setting.

11   Gurri, M. (2024). 'To my friends across the political divide', Discoursemagazine.com. 2 January 2024.

12   Birkinshaw, J., Gudka, M. & D'Amato, V. (2021). 'The blinkered boss: how has managerial behavior changed with the shift to virtual working?', *California Management Review*, 63(4), 5–26.

13   Jones, S. (2022). 'Morgan Stanley's CEO is pushing for a return to the office and says employees need to give up on "Jobland" and focus on "Careerland"', *Business Insider*, 8 March 2022.

Chapter 5

1   The smaller competitors in fact gained the acronym BUNCH: Burroughs, UNIVAC, NCR, Control Data and Honeywell. There were also smaller players in Europe and Japan, all in the shadow of IBM.

2   Mann, Jyoti (2022). 'Meta has spent $36 billion building the metaverse but still has little to show for it', *Business Insider*, 29 October 2022.

3   Stackpole, Thomas (2022). 'What Is Web3?', *Harvard Business Review*, 10 May 2022. https://hbr.org

4   Moravec, Hans (1988). *Mind Children*, Harvard University Press

5   Ray Kurzweil is the most well-known name here. He has predicted 2045 as the year of the singularity. Kurzweil, Ray (2024). *The Singularity Is Nearer*, Penguin.

6   Petzold, B. et al. (2020). 'Designing data governance that delivers value', McKinsey, June 2020.

7   https://www.melconway.com/Home/Conways_Law.html

Chapter 6

1   Friedman, T.L. (2017). *Thank You for Being Late: An Optimist's Guide to Thriving in the Age of Accelerations*, Picador USA.

2   Moore, G.E. (1965). 'Cramming More Components onto Integrated Circuits. Proceedings of the IEEE', 86(1): 82–4.

3   *Forbes Magazine* did this analysis, many have commented on it. For example: Thierer, A. (2009). 'On measuring technology diffusion rates', Techliberation.com, 28 May 2009.

4   Kotter, John P. (1996). *Leading Change*, Boston: Harvard Business School Press. Professor John Kotter wrote a well-known book, *Leading Change*, in which he stated that roughly 70 per cent of the programmes he had been involved with fail to achieve their desired outcomes. Another book – *Re-engineering the Corporation* (Hammer, Michael, & James Champy (2009). Zondervan) – came up with a statistic that between 50 and 70 per cent of change programmes did not quite work out, but neither of these were systematic analyses. They were rule-of-thumb observations from people with genuine expertise but also quite a lot of self-interest in persuading executives that change is difficult.

5   See the Kotter book noted above in 51.

6   Lafley, A.G. & Martin, Roger L. (2013). *Playing to Win: How Strategy Really Works*, Boston, Massachusetts: Harvard Business Review Press.

7   This case study was published in 2018 by London Business School Publishing: The UK Government Digital Service, by Julian Birkinshaw & Scott Duncan. https://publishing.london.edu

8   *The Economist* (2020). 'The Sad Tale of Britain's Government Digital Service', *The Economist*, 29 October 2020. https://www.economist.com

9   This case study was published by London Business School Publishing: Refinitiv: A private equity-led transformation, by Julian Birkinshaw and David Craig, 2022 https://publishing.london.edu

10 Grant, Adam M., Campbell, Elizabeth M., Chen, Grace, Cottone, Keenan, Lapedis, David & Lee, Karen (2007). 'Impact and the Art of Motivation Maintenance: The Effects of Contact with Beneficiaries on Persistence Behavior', *Organizational Behavior and Human Decision Processes* 103 (1): 53–67.

CHAPTER 7

1   Watters, Audrey (2023). *Teaching Machines*, MIT Press.

2   Lohr, S. (2021). 'What ever happened to IBM's Watson?', *New York Times*, 16 July 2021.

3   Zuboff, Shoshana (2019). *The Age of Surveillance Capitalism*, Profile Books.

4   Suleyman, M. (2023). 'My new Turing test would see if AI can make 1 million', *MIT Technology Review*, 14 July 2019.

5   Other popular text-based generative AI products include Claude from Anthropic and Bard from Google. There are also generative AI applications for coding, images, speech and video. For a useful overview of the emerging landscape see: https://www.sequoiacap.com/article/ generative-ai-a-creative-new-world/

6   Frankfurt, Harry G. (2005). *On Bullshit*, Princeton University Press.

7   McKinsey & Co. (2023). 'The state of AI in 2023: a breakout year'.

8   Armstrong, K. (2023). 'ChatGPT: US lawyer admits using AI for case research', www.bbc.co.uk, 27 May 2023.

9   This quote comes from a talk Arka Dhar gave at London Business School in June 2023.

10 National Institute of Economic and Social Research (2022). 'Productivity in the UK: Evidence review (2022)', National Institute of Economic and Social Research, 23 June 2022.

11 Arnal, Elena, Wooseok, O.K. & Torres, Raymond (2003). 'Knowledge, work organization and economic growth'. In *Internet, Economic Growth and Globalization: Perspectives on the New Economy in Europe, Japan and the USA*, pp. 327–76. Berlin, Heidelberg: Springer Berlin Heidelberg, 2003.

12 Upwork (2024). 'From burn-out to balance: AI enhanced work models', Upwork.com, 23 July 2024.

13 https://deepmind.google/research/breakthroughs/alphago/

14 Murray, A. & Gordon, N. (2024). 'Jeff Bezos says his Blue Origin company is exploring space to protect Earth and keep "the natural world" from backsliding', Yahoo Finance, 1 March 2024.

15 Johnson, M. (2017). 'When it comes to investing, human stupidity beats AI', *Financial Times*, 10 April 2017.

16 Roose, K. (2024). 'The data that powers AI is disappearing fast', *New York Times*, 19 July 2024.

17 Jackson, S. (2023). 'The CEO of the company behind AI chatbot ChatGPT says the worst-case scenario for AI is lights out for all of us', *Business Insider*, 4 July 2023.

18 PWC (2016) 'Will robots really steal our jobs?' URL: www.pwc.com/ hu/hu/kiadvanyok/assets/pdf/impact_of_automation_on_jobs.pdf

19 Kelly, J. (2023). Goldman Sachs predicts 300 million jobs will be lost or degraded by artificial intelligence. Forbes.com. 31 March 2023.

20 Ip, G. (2017). 'We survived spreadsheets, and we'll survive AI', *Wall Street Journal*, 2 August 2017.

21 Autor, D. (2024). 'AI could actually help rebuild the middle class', Noema (noemamag.com), 12 February 2024.

22 Kahn, Jeremy (2024). *Mastering AI*, Simon & Schuster.

23 Aoun, Joseph (2018). *Robot-Proof: Higher Education in the Age of Artificial Intelligence*. Cambridge, Massachusetts: The MIT Press.

24 Harari, Y.N. (2016). *Homo Deus: A Brief History of Tomorrow*, Harvill Secker.

25 Naisbitt, John (1982). *Megatrends*. New York.

Afterword

1 Murray, A. & Gordon, N. (2023). 'MIT digital innovation guru says Walmart and JP Morgan are losing the battle against start-ups: "Continuing to exist is a really low bar"', *Fortune Magazine*, 12 November 2023.

2 This widely-quoted statement from Keynes comes from his Galton lecture at the Eugenics Society in 1937.

3 Bennett, Alan (2004). *The History Boys*, Faber and Faber.

INDEX

Note: page numbers in **bold** refer to diagrams. Page numbers in *italics* refer to information contained in tables.